Holly {WOULD}

You Can Be Confident Too!

HOLLY ROUSH

HollyWould
© 2012 by Holly Roush

Published by Insight Publishing Group
4739 E. 91st Street, Suite 210
Tulsa, OK 74137
918-493-1718

ISBN: 978-1-890900-71-7

Printed in the United States of America

What leaders are saying about Holly Roush and her book:

"I am privileged to call Holly my friend. Her personal and professional leadership make me proud to offer my highest recommendation of *HollyWould*. I believe this book will not leave you the same way it found you. You will be inspired and challenged to grow to a higher level of living. The wisdom and passion of Holly's life is contagious and inspires thousands to live up in a sometimes down world."

—Rex Crain
Speaker, life coach, and author of *Life Lift*

"Holly Roush is a great example to women and anyone who wants to become more confident. Her story of a stay-at-home mom to the pinnacle of success will inspire you to believe that anyone with a dream and the willingness to chase that dream can achieve their loftiest goals. She is a make-it-happen person who I've seen firsthand live life the right way. This book is full of great ideas any person can use no matter where they are starting from. I highly recommend it!"

—Dallin Larsen
Founder and CEO of MonaVie
Ernst & Young Entrepreneur of the Year 2009

"Holly Roush is contagious. You are about to catch a case of confidence like you've never had before. When you get around her story and the lessons she lives by, you will be infected with life-changing ideas and inoculated from self-doubt once and for all. I love this book! I highly recommend it."

—John Mason
Author of *An Enemy Called Average* and
numerous other national best-selling books

"Holly is relentless in her pursuit for success and her joy for sharing it. Her energy and practical insight into building a business and succeeding are a must read and a great road map for those who want to emulate her truly amazing story."

—Maria Fiorini Ramirez
President and CEO of Maria Fiorini Ramirez, Inc.
Speaker, global economic consultant,
regular guest on CNBC, CNN, ABC, Fox News,
Bloomberg Financial, and CBS

"I have had the privilege of knowing Holly since 1997. I have seen her go from pharmaceutical rep, to stay-at-home mom, and finally to a business superstar. She has been successful in all three because of her focus, determination, and ability to build loyal personal relationships. I have no doubt that her story will inspire readers to reach heights they never dreamed possible."

—Bo Van Pelt
PGA Tour professional golfer

Dedication

To my mother, a single mom who raised three amazing kids. Without your guidance that pushed me to excel, I would not be where I am today. I am so thankful for you!

To my sister, Carrie. You have been my rock, always standing up for me. You are completely loyal to me and our family. Thanks to you and Bo for sharing the amazing juice opportunity! Who knew the sky would be our limit through a bottle of purple juice? Because you cared enough to share with us, thousands of people have been positively affected, both physically and financially.

To my amazing husband, Corbin. You have put up with so much! On days when I could work 24/7, you keep me in balance by reminding me of what is important: God first, family second, and our business third. You are an amazing husband and father! I'm so thankful to be working alongside you!

To my three amazing, incredibly thoughtful boys, Dakota, Drake, and Ethan. I know my work isn't always easy on you, but you handle it in stride. You boys are always so encouraging to me! Thank you for being sensitive to others, motivating and encouraging them. Set your dreams high! You can achieve greatness by staying faithful, motivated, and working hard.

To my sweet dad with all your spunkiness. I know I definitely got my social skills from you, the man who is always the life of the party. Thanks for all you do!

I love all of you!

Contents

Acknowledgments

I've always believed in the value of a great team, and a book like this could never have come together without the cooperative effort of the following people:

Thank you to my many friends and colleagues who encouraged me to write this book. You nudged me out of my comfort zone and I'm very thankful you did.

Thank you especially to Katie Dobbs, Laura Lester, Jill Noble, Heidi Rodrick, Dan and Maranda Williams, and Emily Wilson for your candid and hilarious interviews. Your thoughts and stories have greatly enriched this book.

A special thanks to Linda Mason for her conscientious and skillful assistance in the writing and editing of this book.

Thank you Jesse Reich, Olivia Lee of Liv Glamorous, and Rachelle Liljenquist for my wonderful pictures, makeup, and hair.

Thank you, Insight Publishing Group, for helping to make a dream come true.

To every man and woman
who dreams scared.

Butter Spreads Some Good News

{ CHAPTER 1 }

"What? I can't hear you, Holly!"

"Sorry! I'm talking to you from my bedroom closet! I'll try to speak up."

To keep the peace in my marriage, I was building my new business from the best hiding place I could find—my small walk-in closet, surrounded by a rainbow of shoes, shirts, and shorts. My sister, Carrie, and her husband, Bo, had just told me about a nutritious product that I thought would interest my friends—like me, they were fitness-conscious moms who were eating well and trying to get their children to do the same. Among them, I was known as the one who enjoyed organizing our get-togethers.

"You'll never believe what Bo and Carrie have stumbled across. An all-natural, antiaging juice made from one of the world's greatest superfoods! I've decided to go into the juice business, and I want my friends to come with me. It's nutritious for our children and we'll have fun making a little money together. If you sign up now, you'll benefit from everyone who joins me later. I don't want you to miss out!"

"Okay, what do I need to do?"

"I need your credit card information, so come on over now and I'll help you join."

My business started in September 2005 when my brother-in-law's phone rang. It was Butter, his childhood friend. Knowing that Bo was a professional golfer on the PGA Tour, he said, "Bo, I've got a product that I think you'll love. It'll help your golf game. Check it out!"

After listening to his friend talk about the juice, Bo recognized its worth nutritionally and as a possible business opportunity for Carrie and me. He knew that we sisters were always dreaming of owning our own business. Once, we dreamed of opening a clothing store; we'd even chosen the name, the paint color, and the clothes! Another time, we dreamed of opening a restaurant, and again, we'd gone as far as choosing the name. Later with a friend, we wanted to go to the world's largest wholesale merchandise mart called the Dallas Market Center, but we couldn't get in unless we had a resale business. To be funny, my husband, Corbin, said, "Start a business called Two Sisters and a Friend!" We actually loved it, so we drove to the courthouse and formed an LLC by that name. We promptly went to Market, where I bought furniture that I ended up selling to my friends at wholesale.

But this time, over dinner at my house, Bo and Carrie shared the juice idea.

Carrie said, "Four ounces of this drink is equivalent to thirteen servings of fruit and provides thirty times the antioxidants of red wine!"

Bo said, "The juice is made out of the açaí berry. I think this is something you'll want to look into. Growing up, I knew people who did so well in this type of business that they lived in mansions in Phoenix and Florida."

Over the years I had learned that Bo had great business sense, so I trusted him. Still, I hesitated because I was now a busy stay-at-home mom raising three active sons: Dakota, age nine; Drake, age six; and Ethan, age three. I wasn't actively looking for a business to run—I was running the household by day and running to football practice at night! My husband, Corbin, had a great job, so we didn't need more money, or so I thought.

What we really needed was freedom from the rat race and the "Go! Go! Go! mentality" that prevented us from spending quality time together. Little did we know, this business could lead us to a lifestyle we had only imagined.

After reflecting some more, I thought, This sounds like a great product! My kids need it. My friends need it. I love people, and this would be a great way to help them!

Eyeing my sister, I said, "If we get territories, Oklahoma is *mine*."

Mind you, Carrie lived only a mile up the road from me, so she said, "This is *my* opportunity, too."

"Hey, your husband's a PGA golfer. He's got his business. Give this one to me."

Carrie started laughing and said, "We won't have territories, Holly. It's one of *those* things."

"One of *what* things?"

"Network marketing."

I joked, "Woo-hoo! That's just what I've been searching for my whole life!"

Overhearing our conversation, Corbin quickly emerged from the kitchen pantry, slamming the door shut. "No way! You are not gonna be the juice lady. All our friends will run from you. You're not getting involved."

Wide awake

After hearing about the juice, I had a problem. For three nights, I couldn't sleep. For three days, I kept walking to my computer and researching all I could find about it. I couldn't believe what I was reading! People were reporting better sleep, increased energy, relief from aches and pains, and better focus and clarity. I asked Bo for Butter's phone number, and Butter gave me the number of a guy named Devon. When I reached him, he was watching an NFL game, so he handed the phone to his girlfriend, Sarah.

"Sarah, I've been researching online, but I don't understand the compensation plan. Tell me how it works and how to put people in."

"I don't know, Holly, but I'll give you the names of two people who do. I regret that I waited two weeks to join because thousands of people got in ahead of me. Get in as soon as you can!"

For three days, I called Carrie and said, "Hurry up and get in so I can get in. Give them your credit card information. If you don't, I'm going to get in before you do."

While I was waiting, I bounced the idea off my trainer at the gym. "I've been researching a nutritional product that I think could potentially be a good business opportunity for you. Since your clients ask you what they should eat, I think you would feel comfortable telling them about it."

He said, "I'm open. Why not supplement my income?"

I decided to jump in; I would help my family and friends, and make a hundred dollars a week to treat myself to manicures and pedicures. Since I wouldn't have to ask Corbin for the money, I wouldn't feel guilty spending it on myself.

I told Corbin, "You know that juice?"

"Yeah, what?"

"It keeps tugging at my heart. I think I'm going to do it."

He said, "Fine, you can do it. But only one night a week. You get one night a week, your girls' night out, your Bunco, your gossip, whatever you girls do. You can keep whatever you make. And in three months, you'll quit, and I'll never have to hear about this again."

Since *I* never wanted to hear *that* again, I quickly reminded myself of a saying I love and completely believe: "The best revenge is total success."

Holly{WOULD}
Act on her personal convictions!

I knew I was never going to have to hear, "Hey, you failed; I told you so." I was going to make it work—a hundred dollars a week!

Forty-eight hours

Maybe I was having a blonde moment when I thought the company Web site commanded me to enroll two people within two days or they would kick me out. "In forty-eight hours, put someone on the left, and someone on the right [sides of your team]."

Thankfully, that sense of urgency launched my business.

Immediately, I got on the phone and I did what every daughter would do. I called my dad. "Hey, Dad, you're unhealthy! You need to drink this product. I need your credit card because I don't want to get kicked out." And I signed up my dad.

Then I called my trainer and said, "Okay, I'm in! I need your credit card information. I've been paying you, so it's time for you to pay me. Let's tell everybody about it!" And I signed up my trainer.

I called three or four friends and said, "Hey, I've been thinking about going into a juice business, and I've decided to do it. My husband says I get one night a week, and I'm pretty sure your husband will say the same. If we just get out there and do this thing together, we can meet every week with all our friends. And we can make some money and get healthy at the same time!"

I signed up five people that first week—my dad, trainer, and three friends. One of the friends was a neighbor named Jill and the two others, Julie and Katie, were moms I had met at school through our kids.

The funny thing was, I hadn't yet tasted the juice because I was waiting for my shipment to arrive. But I had read that it tasted like berries with chocolate overtones, so I thought, I'm good!

The day three cases showed up on my doorstep, I opened them to find the juice packaged in beautiful glass bottles, looking like fine wine. Thank goodness, it tasted wonderful!

Nothing to hide

"I don't want you on the phone all the time," Corbin said.

But I couldn't help it—my phone was ringing off the hook! Those five friends were excited to tell me how the product was helping them and their friends, and I wanted to hear all of their stories.

I hid in the bathroom, the closet, and the bushes outside—anywhere I hoped Corbin wouldn't catch me on the phone. I talked while my sons napped, attended school, and after they went to bed at night instead of watching every reality show on TV.

Holly {WOULD}
Think "outside the office."

The stories I heard were so amazing that I thought, How *can't* I tell people about this juice?

I really felt like I owed everyone I knew the chance to drink it, so I sat down and wrote a list of everybody I could think of. My goal was to call two or three new people every single day.

To my amazement, I didn't make a hundred dollars that first week—I made four hundred eighty!

Dallas, here we come!

Because my friends had thought enough of me to share their credit card information and join me in business, I thought I should think enough of them to learn how we could succeed together. I made that commitment.

After I had been in the business about three weeks, I Googled one of the names Sarah had given me and clicked on his Web site. There I saw an announcement for a company meeting where he was speaking in Dallas, Texas, and the contact number of a man named Tim. I called him and asked if I could attend, and he said yes.

Only two friends, Laura and Julie, would drive down there with me, but we drove the four hours to listen to a man named Brig Hart. We were excited to learn more and to meet all the people in this business in Dallas!

When we arrived in the Hilton hotel ballroom, we were surprised to see only fifteen to twenty people in the room, including the three of us.

Now, this is where most people would have run out the door, thinking, I'm not doing this weird thing—nobody else is doing it.

But I thought, Oh my gosh, no one's doing this in Dallas, Texas? Our opportunity is huge!

Holly{WOULD}
Flip conventional thinking.

As I listened to the speaker, I realized he was in this business to help people, confirming my reason for getting in. I wrote down everything he said in a notebook. He was engaging and fired up! He made us feel like we could succeed. We could tell that he believed what he said, and one thing he said was, "I'm going to help ten people become millionaires this year."

From the front row, I raised my hand and said, "Pick me, pick me!"

He looked over and laughed. When the meeting ended, I asked him, "What will it take to get you to speak in Tulsa?" I was thinking, If I can get Brig's energy and excitement in front of my friends—done deal!

He said, "Who's your upline?"

I thought, What's an upline? I said, "I don't know. I've talked to some guy named Butter and I've talked to some guy named Devon who gave me the names Charlie and Debbie Kalb."

He said, "Oh my gosh, Charlie and Debbie are good friends of mine, so you must be on our team."

"Cool!"

He said, "Fifty people. You get fifty people and I'll come to Tulsa."

Turning to my friends, I said, "We have to put fifty people in this business. We're getting that man to Tulsa to do a meeting for us!"

More excited than ever, on the road home we called and enrolled several people!

Ready, set, hike!

Football in Oklahoma is big. Practically from the day a baby boy takes his first step, his parents strap him in shoulder pads and a helmet.

In September, Corbin was coaching Dakota's third grade team. We were attending practice three nights a week, so I thought, How in the world am I going to do this business now?

Then it occurred to me: Guess who's at football practice? Every parent! And they were all lined up in their lawn chairs for two hours straight.

Opportunity!

Back from Dallas for only three hours, Julie and I brought some SpongeBob Dixie cups and our juice bottles to practice. Pouring some for every parent, we said, "Taste this, and let us know what you think."

Some grabbed their lawn chairs and moved to the other side of the field. Others stayed and asked, "What is this?"

"Four ounces is equivalent to thirteen servings of fruit. Not only is it incredibly good for you, but you can make some money—we just got back from Dallas where we met a man who's making a crazy amount! We're going to do this business together, and we want you to do it with us. But if you don't decide to do the business part of it, that's no big deal. Even if you just drink the juice, you owe it to your family and friends to tell them about its nutritional value. Would you like to hear more about it?"

Some did.

"Great!" I said. "We're having a party Wednesday night at my house. Come and learn more!"

We didn't take ourselves seriously; we were just out on that football field laughing with people, having fun.

Of that initial group of parents, four became very successful in the company, each making two- to five-thousand dollars a week. Why did they join us? They saw how excited we were. We didn't know a ton, but we believed in our product. And that's how our business exploded.

I started taking those juice bottles everywhere I went.

Going purple

I love to shop.

I started thinking, What if I made five hundred dollars every week? With that amount of money, I could do a lot of shopping! Since I started making that amount almost immediately, I started spending it as fast as I could. The company had issued me a purple Visa card that they deposited my earnings onto every week. Every Friday, they sent me the best e-mail of my week: "You've got money!"

In January, I said, "Hey Corbin, let's go to Scottsdale for four or five days. We can watch Bo in a golf tournament and go shopping. I'm going to pay for the whole trip on my purple card."

I could tell he was thinking, "Yeah, right," but he flew there with me.

Have you seen the movie *Pretty Woman* where Julia Roberts plays a character named Vivian? In a poignant scene, Vivian, dressed provocatively as a prostitute, enters a store on Rodeo Drive and asks for help in changing her style. Although the store assistants worked on commission, they hurt her feelings by telling her she's in the wrong place and asking her to leave. At a different store the next day, Vivian spends thousands of dollars on a completely new wardrobe. She returns to the first store looking gorgeous in an elegant dress, hat, and shoes and carrying shopping bags full of her purchases. One of the rude assistants doesn't even recognize her, and Vivian tells her, "I was in here yesterday. You wouldn't wait on me. *Big mistake.*"

I had always wanted to reenact that scene, so with my arms loaded all the way up with shopping bags from several stores, I walked through an exclusive Scottsdale store smiling, but telling an assistant, "You should have helped me!"

Back in our hotel room, my weary arms dropped all the bags from Saks, Louis Vuitton, Nordstroms, and Neiman Marcus on the floor. Wide-eyed, Corbin said, "How much did you spend?"

"It doesn't matter because I bought it all with my purple card."

He said, "Wow! This is pretty cool."

Shopping in New York City during the holidays and trying on expensive jewelry and watches, feeling like a Pretty Woman, 2006.

Surprise!

A few weeks later and six months after I started, I made it to the Diamond level, which at the time was the second highest level that people in our company dreamed of achieving. Even though I had reached this status, Corbin didn't know exactly how much I was making.

One day I told him, "Hey, I'm starting to feel a little guilty. You know we had this deal, and it was a great deal, that whatever I made I got to keep. But that was because I thought I would only make a hundred dollars a week. I think it's time I start helping pay our family's bills."

He said, "Great. Our boys eat a ton of food. You can buy them groceries."

I laughed because a Diamond makes two to four thousand a week. I could pay for a little more than groceries.

I said, "You know what? I called and found out what we owe on my car. How about I pay that off?" Then I handed Corbin a check for seventeen thousand dollars.

In an about-face, Corbin said, "You know what? I'm glad you're doing this. Keep paying off our bills. You can go out every night of the week. You go, girl!"

He suddenly wanted me to run with it! Then he added, "But you can't talk to my friends." A lot of his friends' wives were building the business with me, and he wanted me to leave his friends out of it. Corbin didn't want them calling him "Berry Boy."

All of a sudden I realized, We can become financially free! I changed my goals from a hundred dollars a week for manicures and pedicures, to five hundred dollars a week for shopping, to thousands of dollars a week for complete financial freedom.

After paying off some bills, I earned a company trip called "Diamond Destination" to Costa Rica. In June, Corbin flew with me. I'm going to let him tell you his side of the story.

Corbin's Conversion

{ C H A P T E R   2 }

I went kicking and screaming to Costa Rica. No part of me wanted to hang out with people I thought were only interested in getting me to sign up and buy their products.

I thought, I'll go but I'll mostly hang out by myself.

On the second day of the trip, I told Holly, "I'm just gonna go sit up at the pool bar."

She said, "You just go do that. You go pout, and I'll hang out with my new friends."

After I sat down on a bar stool, I winced when I noticed a man next to me wearing a visor advertising Holly's company. I introduced myself, and discovered his name was Steve Merritt.

I said, "Oh, you're in that juice thing, too?"

He said, "Yeah."

"Well, how's your wife doing in it?"

Fatal mistake.

"My wife! Are you kidding me? This is a man's business. As a matter of fact, this is a couple's business. In Florida where I'm from, we build this thing together. You know, I've heard of you. You must be that fool married to Holly Roush."

Surprisingly, I didn't get mad at him. I had come to the point where I could see the truth. I had started catching my wife in the closet talking on the phone because she was afraid to upset me. Looking inward, I knew I didn't want her to have to do that, so I had told her, "Hey, I'm on board with this deal. I don't mind doing a little bit of babysitting." But, when she worked the couple of nights a week that I allowed, I welcomed her home to the sight of me reclining in an easy chair with my arms defiantly crossed and three unbathed, unfed boys up past their bedtimes running around like Tasmanian devils.

That week in Costa Rica I got to know the guys and their families and friends in Holly's company. I had dreaded meeting the kind of people who wanted to con me and their friends into buying a bunch of junk we didn't need. Instead, I met unified couples who were building their businesses with their children. I listened as the men explained their hearts' desire and vision for their company and I learned how they had built it by helping people financially, relationally, and even spiritually, rather than by taking advantage of them. Not only had their friends joined with them in business, but I noticed and admired their strong bonds of friendship.

Startled, I realized, They have the same dreams, the same types of friends, the same morals, and the same values as mine. I wanted to introduce them to my friends—too bad my friends weren't there!

I was embarrassed by my actions! Holly had a desire and a dream in her heart. From my own little comfortable spot in life, I had made fun of my wife who wanted more.

That's when I said, "Holly, I'm missing out on something."

Holly felt it, too. Our hearts wanted what our new friends had. Holly and I agreed, "Wouldn't it be cool to get all of our friends involved in a business where we could hang out with each other, and our children could be friends with their children for the rest of their lives?"

I was now ready and willing to join my wife.

I flew back to Tulsa with a new fire. I truly understood what it means to be on board, and it isn't babysitting. It means truly taking your future into your own hands, no longer relying on some guy in an ivory tower to decide how much you are worth; a guy who can come and cut you at any time he wants!

Corbin's defining moment: fishing on a boat with other men from around the country who had a dream and a vision for our company.

Golden handcuffs

For fourteen years, I worked for a boss whom I considered a father to me after the death of my own. Less than three months after the Costa Rica trip, he came to me and said words to this effect: "I love you and your family, but you're making too much money for Tulsa, Oklahoma, and I've got to cut you a little bit. Corbin, I'm cutting you by two-thirds. You have three options: one, you can start your own company and I'll bury you; two, you can walk around with that sad look on your face and I'll fire you; or three, you can put a smile on your face, get out there, and sell."

I was stunned. The company was financially sound with no debt, running great, and growing like crazy. And I was the man bringing in over 50 percent of the company's sales.

Holly and I were closing on a lake house the next morning. In a panic, I called her and said, "You've got to cancel everything. Cancel the boat, the house, and the furniture."

I'm not bashing owners or corporate America. When their name is on the door, they have every right to do what they want. They can cut benefits including pensions, commissions, and insurance. Therefore, I don't blame my boss for what he did.

I tried to make that job work. I stayed there for two more months, but I became very unhappy working for a third of my pay. No longer did I feel the worth I once enjoyed.

Why change a good thing?

When Holly told me she wanted to join a juice business, I didn't intend to treat her the way a mean, abusive husband would when I set constraints on her.

It's just that she was rocking our comfort level.

I had a great job, making lots of money. And for Tulsa, Oklahoma, we had nice cars and a nice home. Our kids attended private school. We were in the perfect spot that people dream of achieving after they get out of school. Life was great.

So for us to be in that perfect spot when Holly shared with me her desire to start this kind of marketing, something that I had run from and didn't want any part of, I felt like she'd hit me in the gut.

Didn't she think I had provided well enough for her and our boys? Wasn't our lifestyle good enough? Why did she want to complicate it? Corporate America required lots of hours from me including some international travel, so when I came home at night my goal was family time. I knew that once Holly got on board and started running with her new idea, she would devote time to it that I didn't want stolen from our family.

I said, "We need to have some barriers in our life. We need to control this thing a little bit." And she agreed to my restrictions.

She and a couple of friends drove to Dallas to hear a speaker by the unusual name of Brig, and afterward, she went out and ran with it more than ever while I stood back on the sidelines and watched. Speaking of sidelines, I couldn't believe what I saw one day coaching football at our sons' Christian school. In the huddle, one of my assistants said, "Hey, Corbin, why is your wife over on the sidelines pouring wine for everybody?"

Dakota's third grade football team after a game in 2005.

Looking over there, I saw Holly and one of her friends running up and down the sidelines pouring that juice.

I thought, Oh my gosh, I don't know who that Brig guy is, but I'm gonna kill him!

A lot of the time, I wasn't happy with her. I got irritated because I felt the stress of working for somebody else; I had sales to achieve and quotas to reach. In the evenings I was on the phone, conducting overseas business with China, Taiwan, Hong Kong, and Korea.

Nervous about losing family time, I thought of Holly's business as a complication. I was willing to let her run with it, but I didn't want any part of it. Never personally experiencing her new industry, and never hearing of anyone who achieved any success in it, I was a little embarrassed and shied away.

When Holly started experiencing tremendous success, instead of feeling proud of her accomplishments, I was blown away and jealous. Why had I worked all of those long hours for someone else in a job that was beating me down? Compared to all the hours and years I had worked to achieve my success, I was irritated that she had achieved so much, so quickly.

Both of us were working for companies that were doing great financially, but my company was looking for ways to cut corners and reduce compensation to their sales force, while Holly's company was receptive to and implementing new ways to put more money into her pocket.

To top it off, she was going out and having a great time, building a business with friends and family. Every time I was around them, they were always excited, always smiling.

Changing my mind

Around the time Holly and I flew to Scottsdale, Arizona, for her shopping spree, she showed me how to log online to her business account.

I'll never forget that day because back in my office in Tulsa, I had a bunch of customers calling in. Even though I was on vacation, I called the office and checked my voice mail. I got to hear my customers complaining that their work wasn't getting done in my absence; their orders weren't being placed and the sales weren't going out the door. Nobody back at the office was doing the things I normally did.

Out of curiosity, I logged on to Holly's business site and found her new distributor report. A lot of people were joining. Her business was growing like crazy, and my business back in Tulsa was slowing down and coming to a complete halt because I wasn't there to do it.

It dawned on me, Here I am in Scottsdale, Arizona, trying to take a vacation, but my work's piling up beyond belief and I'm dreading taking care of it when I come home. Holly has put people into her business and then helped them turn around and do the same, so where is she now? Out shopping, having the time of her life!

My wife had the best deal.

Her business model was beautiful. Mine was capped. I could only do so much because there are only so many hours in a day. All I could do to make more money in my job was trade more time away from my family. All of our just-married dreams of nice homes, nice cars, giving to our church, retiring at fifty-five, and being financially free had come to a screeching halt because there was only so much I could do on my own. I had a financial ceiling, while the sky was Holly's limit!

So when Holly put thousands of dollars of purchases on her purple card in Scottsdale, the proverbial lightbulb went on in my head: Wow, I've got something here that could potentially be pretty big!

I was still uncomfortable with getting out of my comfort zone to share juice as a networker, but I realized I could help grow Holly's business another way. I called some of my friends and told them, "You need to get your wife to listen to what my wife has going on." At the time, I still thought it was just a business for women.

When I went to Costa Rica, I got to hear the amazing company vision from the owner himself. From a corporate standpoint, I was fascinated to hear a man who had a vision already in place to take his business not only to a billion dollars, and not only to five-billion dollars, but to twenty-billion dollars in sales. He had the foundation and he knew what he needed to do. And it was so refreshing to hear a man whose vision included giving back to his distributors. He said he could never pay a distributor too much—he would never set a cap.

I'll never forget coming home from that trip, realizing what my wife had her hands on. With renewed dreams, I thought, Through this opportunity, wouldn't it be incredible if we could retire at fifty? Knock five years off.

What if we ran with this business as hard as we could?

With excitement and energy, I put together a list of every single successful person I knew. I didn't care what they did, and I didn't prejudge whether or not they would be interested in the opportunity I wanted to run by them.

What if Holly and I could get them doing a little bit, and help them find some friends who could do a little bit? I wanted to show them how their income potential would go through the roof.

So that's what we did.

Holly and I started dreaming together again. We even thought, Hey, maybe we can retire at forty-five, or maybe even forty!

I quit!

It's so interesting that Holly had a vision and a dream of taking this opportunity and running with it as hard as she could. She had dug a well, one we didn't realize we would soon need. Now, we had a plan B.

On October 1, shortly after my boss gave me his three options, I was able to walk in and give him a fourth.

"Hi, do you remember giving me three options?"

"Yes, Corbin. Come on in and sit down."

"Well, I have a fourth. I'm going to resign and go to work with my wife."

"What does she do? She's a stay-at-home mom."

"She sells juice."

"That will never work. Call me when it's over if you want your job back."

November 1 was my last day on that job. At age thirty-eight, I retired from the corporate world. After forbidding my wife to become the juice lady, I was now officially "The Juice Guy" of Tulsa.

I want you to know, it was the best thing that ever happened to me, and on many levels. If Holly hadn't had the confidence to act on her personal convictions, I don't know where we'd be right now.

Thank God she did.

Friends Do What Friends Do

{ C H A P T E R   3 }

One afternoon in September, my neighbor, Jill, pulled into my driveway to drop my oldest son off from school. I greeted her with a bottle of juice in my hands.

"Jill, I keep leaving messages on your recorder. Come on, you need to do this with us. It's not going to hurt you just to drink the product. Get in and then we'll decide what to do."

Jill had just started a job she loved, but was working way more hours than she expected.

"Jill, you need to check this out. Just drink it and get your position."

I shook the bottle, poured some, and gave it to her to try.

I said, "Come on, Jill. What if it works?"

"Oh, Holly! Why do you keep talking to me about this? But all right, I don't want to miss out."

So Jill signed up.

Looking back, Jill, a Hawaiian Blue Diamond Executive says, "Holly was so excited when she introduced the juice to me! I said yes only because she was my friend.

"I was thinking, I'm going to stop drinking it in October, and she won't notice. Now, I've reached my six-year anniversary with the company! I would never ever have done this if it hadn't been for her."

Laura

On September 30, Jill turned around and signed up another mom from school, her friend and tennis partner, Laura. Laura had read a book about the benefits of the açaí berry and had been searching for a way to get it. When she signed up, she ordered twelve cases!

Checking my business site, I noticed her order and called Jill immediately. "Oh my gosh, Laura made a huge mistake! She just ordered twelve cases! Can you call her? Her husband is going to kill her when he sees it."

When Jill called Laura, this was her response: "I meant to do that. It's a way better deal at twelve cases than it is at one case. Anybody knows that."

She was so smart! And now she's a Hawaiian Blue Diamond Executive!

From left to right: Holly, Katie, Laura, and Jill.

Katie

On October 5, 2005, Katie signed up. She had battled debilitating fatigue for over a year, so I took her a bottle of juice and set it on her counter. It sat there for two weeks.

In the meantime, she started hearing good things about the juice from our other friends who had started drinking it. She researched the açaí berry and discovered its amazing antioxidant value, so she drank the juice and realized she felt like the Energizer Bunny in only two days. Sitting in her car at her son's soccer practice, she called me. She knew about a company where people join and get the product cheaper, so she said, "Okay, how do I get this cheaper?"

I said, "You need three cases."

"Three cases? I'm the only one that's going to be drinking it. I don't think I need three cases."

"No, you really do because you want to share it with people."

"Well, let me think about it."

I said, "Well, I'm going to have a meeting tomorrow night, so it's better if you get in now because I'm going to be putting other people in, and it's better if you're above them than below them."

Katie said, "Well, how much is three cases?"

I told her and she thought, Whew! My husband's going to kill me, but the stuff works!

Katie said, "Okay, fine."

Before her order arrived, she kept coming over to my house and taking bottles out of my refrigerator; she was telling people how good she felt and they wanted to try it. She went through three cases of juice before she received her three-case delivery! Then she turned around and ordered twelve more cases.

The juice changed her life in more than one way. A former college tennis player, she had quit playing the game because every time she played, her neck and shoulder would hurt and a migraine headache would set in. Eventually, she couldn't even carry in the groceries without arthritis pain. After drinking the product for two weeks, she started noticing a difference in the pain, and after five weeks, Katie was pain free. She is now a Diamond Executive in the business.

Since people were getting results, they didn't want to run out—when they did, it only took two days to feel their aches and pains again—so my friends kept calling me and saying, "Holly, we need another case." I was always ordering twelve cases and meeting my friends while we waited in line for school to dismiss. Our school parking lot became the first distribution center in Tulsa before Tulsa had an official distribution center.

As Katie explains, "That's where a lot of activity was happening for us. We were in line, and bottles were being passed. The backs of the cars would open up and there would be cases of the juice and parents standing there talking. It was a juice-exchange place."

We had fun moving our product!

Emily

That same fall, I met Emily and her husband, Kevin, at a trade show in Tulsa. They were there promoting their gym, and I was there sharing my juice. Our booths were only two apart.

Emily would later say:

Holly bugged us all day long. She kept coming to our booth.

"Try the juice."

Please go away.

"Oh, don't you think you want the juice in your gym? There's a book that talks about the main ingredient, the açaí berry."

Please leave us alone.

"You should do this. You're a nutritionist and this is great nutrition. Why don't you put this in your gym?" Then she gave us information about the juice.

In her eyes, our gym in midtown would provide a needed retail outlet. That way, if people kept calling her at night to try a bottle, she could say, "You can actually go buy it at this location..."

At the end of the day, she left a bottle with us and said, "Just drink it. Two ounces morning and night, and let me call you on Monday and see what you guys think."

My husband said, "I'm busy Monday" and thought she would go away.

Persistent Holly said, "Great! How about Tuesday?"

Kevin said, "Fine. Call us at 9:00 a.m. on Tuesday morning."

She penciled us in for Tuesday morning.

That happened on Friday. Over the weekend, I drank the juice. The second night, I felt better. I felt energetic at times of the day I didn't normally have energy, and I'm a healthy person, so I noticed it.

I said to Kevin, "There's something to this, and I have to find out. What was the name of the book that girl told us about?" I got the book and I read it.

Holly called at exactly nine o'clock Tuesday morning and we signed up. It's been a great relationship ever since, and now we're Blue Diamond Executives.

Teamwork

Whatever your business idea, you will find that there is really no such thing as a self-made man or woman. In every successful enterprise, a team of people that works together builds the business.

Confidence comes from surrounding yourself with a team. Gather your team.

Party Time!
{ C H A P T E R   4 }

After ten to fifteen people signed up, we replaced Bunco night with home juice-tasting parties. In Dallas, Brig had presented the business plan by drawing on a wipe board. Since I had literally written down everything he wrote, when I returned home, guess what I did?

I wrote on my wipe board exactly what he had written, and I started teaching my friends to do the same.

Beginning bloopers

Tastings weren't scary for me because I thought of them as a way to have fun. I told our handful of people to bring more people, and my sister, Carrie, helped me throw a party in my home. The two of us stood up there in front of everyone to talk.

We were horrible.

We butchered the compensation plan. We tried to draw circles the way Brig did, but then we couldn't explain what they meant. We got Sharpie ink on our hands and then suddenly noticed it all over each other's faces.

Since we were at home with our close friends, we all laughed. We figured we were all starting out in this together. We had no idea what we had our hands on; it was a new community commerce business and as we shared our product with everyone, we made money by default.

I simply said, "We'll learn as we grow."

In any new business venture, I think it's easy to lack confidence because you feel like you don't know what you're doing. I understand! Who doesn't feel that way at first?

When someone asks you a question, there's never anything wrong with saying, "You know what, that's a great question! I'll get back to you on that," and then changing the topic to something else.

You don't need to know all the answers right there on the spot. What you don't want to do is just wing it, giving out false information. You can always find the answer and inform someone a little later. All of us learn as our businesses grow, all along the way. Instead of feeling overwhelmed, rest assured that your knowledge will increase over time. The more you experience, the more you will come out on top, feeling confident!

Holly{WOULD}

Learn as business grows.

Sharing the courage

On Laura's way back to Tulsa from our Dallas trip, the first person she signed up was her identical twin sister. I called Laura that first week after the trip and picked her brain about who she knew to help her build her business. We both worked out at the same place and I asked her who she knew there.

Laura identified a person she knew and I said, "Oh my gosh, you have to get in the car right now and take her a bottle."

Laura was uncomfortable about doing it, but she called the gym and asked, "Is Dedee still there?"

"Yes, she's here."

She said to her husband, Jim, "I'm taking a bottle to her right now."

Laura says: "In that moment, Holly gave me the courage. There's no telling how instrumental that was in my psyche for my business. I drove over there, and gave Dedee a bottle. At my first tasting party, I invited Dedee. She brought a friend who also brought a friend, and a friend of mine attended. Holly jumped up there and used a dry erase board. We did everything wrong, but Holly laid the foundation for my business. Dedee enrolled and became the second person I sponsored. She went Blue Diamond in the business. That first week after Dallas, my business really got under way!"

Emily's first tasting

Emily describes it this way:

Holly would get people to meetings however she thought she needed to. She got me to my first tasting by saying, "It's at Carrie Van Pelt's house. You have to come see the house!"

Funny thing, I couldn't care less what people's houses look like, but I said, "Well, fine, I'll go."

Funnier still, at that very first meeting, she made me stand up and talk about the product!

There I was sitting among sixty people, all strangers except my sister-in-law, Samantha, whom I had dragged to that party, when Holly started her spiel. Suddenly I heard her say, "The product is great, but I'm going to have Emily come up and tell you about it because she's a nutritionist and a trainer and she owns a gym down on Brookside. You'll definitely want to hear about the product from her."

I thought, *Great!* I've never even seen a tasting presentation before.

As she sat down, I whispered, *"I don't talk in front of people that I don't know! What do you want me to say?"*

"Well, I'm just thinking because you're a trainer and you know the nutritional side of this product, you can just stand up there and tell them what you think about the product. Just tell them all that stuff you already told me about it."

Holly{WOULD}
Be bold.

I reluctantly stood up and started by telling how I experienced an increase in energy from drinking the antioxidant-rich juice. Then I added something like this: "We all hear that we need more antioxidants, but what I found out is that we can't get enough from the fruit we buy in our grocery stores. In everything we do, we consume energy. The by-product of the oxidation cycle is a free radical which is a cell that has lost an outer electron and has been knocked out of its chemical bond. In a sense, a free radical is a damaged cell in our body that has lost something. It will capture electrons from normal healthy cells and create even more free radicals. Two bad cells become four which become eight, then sixteen, and on into thousands. Until you control a free radical, it will go rampant and form thousands of free radicals which cause inflammation. Inflammation is the base of many diseases, so we have to stop free radicals.

"Antioxidants stop free radicals from reproducing to the point where inflammation occurs by neutralizing them. God made our bodies in a way that they already produce antioxidants, and if we lived in a perfect little world, our bodies would be able to control free radicals. But so many things cause free radicals—processed foods, alcohol, smoke, foods high in fat, lack of sleep, stress—that we need extra antioxidants. So when you drink two ounces of this juice morning and night, you ingest the equivalent of thirteen servings of fruit, and consequently, your antioxidant potency is huge. By drinking this, you're neutralizing free radicals which slows inflammation which slows disease. I'm not saying we're curing, treating, or healing anything, but we're enabling our body to do what God intended it to do."

When I finished, I realized I had talked for fifteen minutes!

What Holly didn't know was that I was the Texas A&M student who put off taking Speech Comm 101 until my very last class! As president of my sorority, I would get up and talk to girls I knew, but I was petrified to talk in front of people I didn't know, or in front of a large group, or with a microphone in my hand.

After that first experience, I started doing tastings with Holly all over the place. Once I talked a few times, it became easier.

Until the day someone wanted to film us.

Holly and I drove to Oklahoma City for the filming, and found ourselves in a long room with about 250 people in it.

Suddenly, I noticed people setting up microphones.

"Holly, why are there microphones here?"

"Oh, because they're filming us in this kind of room with so many people. We have to use microphones to be heard."

I said, "I'm stopping right here. I do not do microphones! I will talk loudly enough for people to hear me."

She just looked at me and said, "You have to use a microphone."

I thought, How? When I talk, my hands move. How was I going to say "antioxidants" with a microphone in my hand?

But I did! And after talking that way a few times, I learned that I was fine with a microphone.

Emily at her first big meeting using a micro-phone at a Marriott hotel in Oklahoma City, August 2006.

With or without a microphone, when Holly told me to get up in front of people and talk, she helped me muster the confidence to talk. It's amazing how Holly can just make people do things.

Holly {WOULD}
Nudge people outside their comfort zones.

Moving on up

As our business grew in Tulsa, I said, "We're going to do hotel meetings and we're going to book every Tuesday night for the next two months. I need people slotted for each meeting."

I asked people to speak who were consistently coming to meetings and growing their businesses.

"Katie, can you speak October 9th?"

"Emily, can you speak the 17th?"

After I booked them, I e-mailed a calendar to everyone.

Emily reflects, "What was unique about people in our business in Tulsa was that we all thought of ourselves as part of the Roush group. We all just kind of looked at this as growing the juice business in this area. It wasn't about 'me'; it was about making people realize this is a great product. We didn't know the terms upline and downline. It didn't matter. We were just all one big group."

Katie remembers: "When we were doing these hotel meetings in Tulsa, it was easy for me to get up and speak for forty-five minutes on the product. But when Holly asked me to do more, I was afraid.

'Katie, you need to be leading the meetings.'

'Holly, I'm not a public speaker.'

'Just tell your story.'

'I'm terrible at drawing the compensation plan.'

'You will know more than anyone else in that room. No one's going to know if you make a mistake. You can do this! And someday this will be your testimony—that you overcame your fear. And people will be inspired by that. You can do this!'"

Going with the flow

As soon as Tuesday night meetings grew to seventy people consistently, I said, "I think we need to do Tuesday *and* Thursday nights."

We started doing Tuesday and Thursday night meetings in the hotel. We always met in the same room. The designated host brought the juice. The designated speaker spoke. We all set up the room ourselves. We stood up there and talked to people and drank the juice.

Then all of a sudden, the meetings dropped down to less than thirty people, so I said, "Now let's go back to one meeting a week."

When the hotel stopped working out well, I said, "Let's go back to our homes," and when we outgrew our homes again, I said, "Let's go back to the hotel."

A lot of people get scared when changes occur. They think, We're not in hotels anymore, so maybe business is going downhill.

I just always flowed according to the trends in the business, and to me, none of it was that big of a deal.

Katie explains, "Holly is fearless. She's not afraid of anything or anybody. She doesn't care about what people think, and she pursues things of value with no fear."

Holly{WOULD}
Pursue value without fear.

A place for everyone

In our meetings, we later added business tools and technical support, giving every personality a place to shine:

High-energy person? Greeter!

Accountant? Ticket-money collector at the door.

New in the business? Pour samples of the product.

Seasoned individuals? Work the tools table.

Techy? Run computer, sound, and slide show.

Confidence comes from using the gifts and abilities God gave you.

Any business has the whole combination it needs when the members of its team work off each other's strengths and weaknesses. Each person in a business doesn't have to be the best in everything; instead, every teammate works with others who are best where he or she is weak.

Holly{WOULD}
Love teamwork!

We started out as a handful of friends and we kept growing.

Money and Madness
{ C H A P T E R   5 }

About two weeks after I met Brig for the first time in Dallas, I called him and said, "Hey, Brig, I have my fifty!"

He said, "Did I say fifty? How about one hundred?"

Most people would have been mad, thinking, That guy told me fifty! But I thought, Fifty people in front of this man would have been huge, but one hundred? *Even bigger!*

Holly {WOULD}
Keep her eyes on the bigger picture.

I told Brig, "I'll get one hundred!"

My team and I went to work, and a few weeks later I called him back.

"We have our hundred!"

He said, "I'm going to send my friends Charlie and Debbie Kalb."

I had never met them, so I had no idea who they were. The day they pulled in from Florida, a friend and I took them to dinner.

Sitting at the table, I said, "Charlie, you have to talk about the product. We don't care about the money because we're in this for fun and we want to get healthy."

He looked at me and said, "Holly, I don't know anything about the product. All I know about is the money. I'm probably not your guy."

Eyes wide, I said, "Well, we have a houseful of people coming to hear you tonight so please just help me out here."

At the party, I was feeling nervous. I was thinking, Oh my gosh, he's going to blow all these people out of the room because he's going to talk money and *we do not talk about money!*

Standing inside our host's million-dollar home, Charlie began by saying, "Holly said y'all are into the product, and I have to tell you, I know nothing about the product. I really don't care about the product because I'm in this for the money. And by looking out there in the driveway and down the street at the Mercedes, BMW, Jaguar, Land Rover, and the Hummer you drove here, I kind of feel like y'all are, too. We're talking money."

Exchanging indignant glances, my teammates and I whispered, "Oh my gosh, can you believe this!"

Afterward, a few people told us they were upset because Charlie talked about money, but it didn't matter because each of them were still excited and wanted to stay in. But Charlie's focus on the financial benefits of the business opened our eyes to a new possibility we hadn't tapped. On the other hand, Charlie said, "Before now, I never realized how much the ladies love the benefits of our product!"

That day, we all discovered what women and men wanted: The women? Make me feel well and look good. The men? Show me the money!

Charlie Kalb speaking to a houseful of people.

It's the president calling!

For some reason, the kids were out of school one morning, so we joined a lot of other parents and their kids at a bowling alley. My cell phone rang, and I noticed an 801 number from Utah on my screen.

"Hello?"

"Holly, this is Dallin Larsen, founder and CEO of the company. How are you?"

I wondered, Have I done something wrong? I gulped and said, "I'm good?"

It was so loud in the bowling alley that I turned and whispered to a couple of moms standing near me, "It's the CEO of the company. I'll be right back. Watch my kids."

I ran to a quieter place and heard Dallin say, "Man, things are going crazy there in Tulsa, Oklahoma. I am so proud of you guys.

What are you doing? Is there anything I can do to help? I would love to book a meeting there. Brig and I are going to come out."

"Wow! Thank you!"

When Corbin came home from work that night, I told him, "You're never going to believe this. The president called me!"

"What does George Bush want from you?"

"Oh, no, I meant Dallin Larsen from the juice company."

"Who cares! Come on, that thing's not gonna last! No one makes any money off that!"

But I thought, How many CEOs would take the time to call and say, "I want to come visit" or "Great job"?

That's when I knew the company executives really cared. They were watching our team, and their recognition got all of us excited and motivated to do more!

Holly {WOULD}

Listen to the top to get to the top.

A taste of Oklahoma

I couldn't wait for the big day!

Up till then, Corbin had never come to any of my meetings. This was our first big tasting event, so I said to him, "You're coming. The CEO of the company is going to be there. Brig Hart, the number-one distributor, is going to be there. I want you there."

He said, "Fine, I'll show up at 7:30 p.m. when the meeting starts."

When Corbin arrived, the line of waiting people was wrapped all the way down the hall to the front door at the Renaissance Hotel. Noticing this as he walked in, Corbin thought, Oh, my gosh, if they're all here for Holly's meeting, we're going to be rich, but it won't last!

When the meeting started, Dallin started handing the microphone around the crowd. A bum who had made his way off the street started screaming into it.

"It's not this juice that's going to save you, it's God. Satan is trying to get you. You're going to hell!"

I was dying. I was thinking, Corbin's in the back thinking I brought this guy as part of the show. Little did I know, Dallin was thinking Brig brought him, and Brig was thinking Dallin brought him. I was thinking they both brought him and now we're dead. One hundred of my closest friends were in that room! I ran onstage and said in Brig's ear, "Get the microphone from him!"

Brig said, "You don't know him?"

Overhearing, Dallin leaned over and said, "You don't know him?"

I said, "I don't know him!"

As Brig tried to take the microphone away, the man started playing tug-of-war. Everyone watched as the two men pulled the mike back and forth. Finally, Brig got it! As he said something to calm everyone down, the man took off out the door. *Gone!*

Dallin will never forget Oklahoma!

Why?

{ CHAPTER 6 }

"Okay, I've been here three times and now it's your turn to come to Florida to one of my meetings."

Fortunately, that first Tulsa meeting with Dallin hadn't stopped Brig from returning a couple more times. When he asked us to return the favor, my friends and I all said, "Sure, we'll come to Florida."

But then, when it came right down to it, Katie was the only one going.

She went home and told her husband, "I'm going to Florida because Brig told me I needed to."

"Brig has a lot more money than you do," he said.

I called Katie and asked, "Are you going to Florida?"

"Yes, I'm going to Florida."

So our first winter in business, we flew together to Florida, stayed in a hotel, and attended our first business function. Corbin hadn't wanted me to go and I knew how mad he was at home. The event was right after Christmas, and I felt very guilty about spending the money to come.

Once there, I saw amazing, loving couples onstage. It was clear that the men adored their wives. These happy couples had a great life in business together! They had what I wanted.

I love the color black!

The second day of the meeting, Dallin said to Brig and his wife, Lita, "We were wondering what to give you when you reached Black Diamond, and we thought, Should we give you a pink Cadillac? No, that's already been done. So we decided on something else."

And Dallin presented them with a shiny, new, black Mercedes convertible! Brig and Lita took it for a spin, and after their ride, Katie and I jumped in the car and started taking pictures of each other!

Sitting in Brig and Lita Hart's brand-new Mercedes in Tampa, Florida, right after it was presented to them in January 2006.

"Oh, wow! I love this car! I've got to have it!" I said.

While everyone was exclaiming, "Oh, I'm so happy for Brig! Aren't you thrilled for Brig," I was interrupting, "How do I get the car? What do I have to do to get the car? Do *you* know what I have to do to get the car?"

No one knew.

I told Charlie, "You have to find out! I've got to get that car!"

I called Corbin and said, "Oh my gosh! They're giving away a Mercedes!"

He said, "No they're not. That's so fake! No company gives away cars like that! They're scamming you. See, they can't even tell you how to get the car!"

But I was laser focused. I wanted that car, and I was going to get it!

Back home from Florida, I called Emily and said, "There's a black Mercedes! We have to have this car!"

I set a new goal: Black Diamond, Black Mercedes.

That August, Corbin's pay was cut by two-thirds and we lost out on moving into our lake house. That same month, the juice company presented me with a brand-new black Mercedes 550SL convertible!

What do you want?

No matter your business idea, to succeed in it you must first determine your "why." A why is a compelling reason and a driving force, and it will give you confidence to keep pursuing your business endeavor.

What's your why?

To discover it, let yourself dream. Do whatever inspires you to dream—sit still and think, take a walk outside, sit in the sun, or maybe get a massage. You'll find your why when you take time to ask yourself, If I could have anything or do anything (in the near or distant future), what would it be?

Maybe it's paying for your child's college education.

Maybe your daughter is getting married and the best dress is five thousand dollars. What if you could buy her that dress?

Maybe you've always envisioned giving big sums of money to your church. What if your church needed ten thousand dollars and it wouldn't be a big deal to supply it?

Would you love to own a house? Look at houses.

Would you love to travel? Look at pictures in a travel book to discover where you want to go.

Holly{WOULD}
Dream big!

Watch things that make your mind think bigger and more creatively.

I told our whole team, "Go to the movie *Just Go With It* starring Jennifer Aniston and Adam Sandler because it was filmed at the Grand Wailea Resort in Maui where the company takes us. Look at that resort—it's dream-building. That's where you could go for free!"

We've watched *Amazing Race* together as a family to show our sons Switzerland because that's where the company is taking us next. I watched *The Bachelor* when it was filmed in Bora Bora and South Africa because the company took us to Bora Bora, and in a couple of years, they're taking us to South Africa.

I tell people, "Nothing on TV compares to what you get to do in the business. If you work for your dreams, you can have them. Create your own reality show."

When we first sat down with Dallin Larsen in Costa Rica, he said, "We will have a company jet, and the leaders will be able to use it to build their business around the country."

Since then, he's done exactly that. He flew into Tulsa on the private jet, picked up Corbin and me, and flew us to a meeting in Dallas. But before we took off, he let two hundred people walk through that plane with their kids, motivating them to think, I'm going to get to do this one day!

If you don't have a dream, life isn't fun. A dream keeps you from quitting.

Dallin Larsen, CEO of the juice company, and his wife, Karree, flew Corbin and me to Dallas to see our team in October 2008.

High-heel why

I remember a day I almost quit. Some family members were questioning my involvement in the business and Corbin was mad I was still involved! That night, I remember lying in bed and praying, "Should I do this? Everyone thinks I'm nuts. Show me why I should do this. I need a sign."

The very next morning I awoke to an e-mail from a stranger who had health issues that made her feet feel tight and hard and her legs ache. She said, "Thank you for sharing a bottle of juice with a person who shared it with me. All of a sudden, my feet went from feeling like boulders to rocks to pebbles, and I was able to wear high heels to my daughter's wedding."

Since I love helping people, I cried. I knew that was my sign!

As long as I know I'm making a positive difference in people's lives, I will keep sharing my product.

Confidence is a willingness to give something you believe in a try, even if it isn't wildly accepted by people you care about.

Later on, Corbin said: "I finally opened my heart and said, 'All right, God. She is so passionate about this and she wants this thing more than I could ever imagine. I need to go support her.' And that's what I did!"

If you don't have a why—something compelling to shoot for—then working hard really isn't worth it. Your why will give you confidence to step out and keep going.

The Power of Two
{ C H A P T E R 7 }

Everyone was calling me, "Can you come to my house? Can you come to my house?"

Corbin only allowed one night a week, so I was being pulled everywhere that one night. I outsmarted him by doing some tastings during the day while he was at work. Even so, I felt like I needed more than one of me.

To duplicate myself, a few of us on our team got together and wrote down the key points to cover in a tasting party. We wrote on simple white flip charts that we reproduced and sold. I knew I couldn't be everywhere, but I knew that flip chart could.

I told people, "All you need to do is get this flip chart and read it. You can do it!"

Whatever your business, when people tell you, "I have to have *you* come down and do this for me," stop! No, you don't. No one did it for me! I started alone. If you do everything for people, you'll drain your energy and deprive them of the opportunity to grow in confidence.

Holly{WOULD}
Duplicate herself.

Laura: "I will tell you, that handmade, laminated, black-and-white flip chart with some misspelled words and incorrect math took me to a million-dollar business! Just a diagram with an outline that gave me the confidence to start doing presentations for my team on my own, it was probably the most important tool that laid the foundation for my business. It was the start of a system."

Two jobs

After Corbin's income was cut, he kept getting up and going to his job, trying to make it work. He counseled with Brig, who told him to make three times his current income before he quit his job.

I advised him to sign up five people to get his name on the business, since originally it was only in my name.

"How do I do it?" he asked.

I said, "Build a list. Contact and invite. That's what Brig's business system says to do."

Corbin said, "Okay, I'm a systems guy. I can follow a system. Just show me what I need to do."

I handed him our business system book called the *MAP* and said, "Go read it."

He said, "All right. I can read."

In any business, following a system builds confidence!

After Corbin read it, he said, "Holly, this thing is so elementary, a third grader could do it." He became a student of the *MAP's* ten-step pattern to success and he signed up five people!

For his job, he was still traveling one week out of every month—sometimes overseas—and the days when he was in town, he was showing up at work first thing in the morning and staying late. He didn't let fatigue become an excuse not to fulfill his why.

Keeping his eye on the goal, he met people in the mornings for coffee, called people on his way to work, called some more during his lunch hour, and talked to even more after work to explain the community commerce opportunity. Some of his friends who initially said no, he called back and said, "Give me your information so I can help you succeed." He came home at night and hung out with the kids. After they went to bed, he called more people. He even talked to every parent at football and basketball practices!

When he met Emily's husband, Corbin said, "That guy has a dream, too. I'm going to align myself with him." Kevin was one of the men in Tulsa flipping the flip chart, and Corbin started calling him to keep himself fired up.

When our business income reached a point where it tripled our income from Corbin's job, I said, "Corbin, you're miserable. You were never this short-tempered. It's time to walk away from your job."

Walking in and resigning was the toughest thing he had ever done because he thought that security meant someone else was paying his insurance and contributing to his 401k.

I was doing a tasting that morning at our house with about thirty people. I was sweating, thinking, Is he going to do it or is he going to chicken out?

My phone rang. I had to make someone else stand up and do the meeting so I could take the call outside. Corbin had chickened out.

"Go back in. You can do it!"

I waited. My phone rang again.

"I did it!"

"Yyyeeeeeesss!"

Retirement

His first morning of retirement, Corbin planned to work out and golf, but first he wanted to sleep till he was done. I wasn't going to let that happen.

"Corbin, you have a tasting this morning."

"What are you talking about? I've never done a tasting."

He'd seen maybe two.

"You're going to flip the flip chart. Just get up there and read what's on the pages."

"I didn't invite anybody."

"We have about twenty women coming over at 10:30."

"Well you're going to be here, aren't you?"

"No, I'm going shopping."

Corbin's Perspective

The women started piling in and they were all so excited. They looked at me and said, "Where's Holly?"

I said, "She's not here today. I'm doing the meeting."

One of them looked at me and said, "I know more than you do."

Nervous, I started reading the first page of the chart. "Nineteen fruits from around the world…" I got it out! I was proud of myself.

I turned around and smiled at the women, but they didn't smile back. I started feeling nervous again.

But when I started reading some of the stuff on that flip chart about the antioxidant powers of the juice, I got excited! "Really? Wow! Think about that!"

And all of a sudden, they started smiling and it became easy.

Behind the scenes

When the women arrived, I pretended to leave the house, but actually I hid in our office and listened to Corbin's presentation.

"Wel…come…A…gift…from…the…Amazon…"

I imagined bewildered looks on the ladies' faces, and heard one of them mimic him by slowly reading the copyright information on the bottom of the first page.

One woman said, "I could do this better than you."

Corbin said, "If I'm so bad, then why aren't you in your own home, flipping your own chart?"

I'm not going to lie. Corbin had seen a tasting party only a couple times and he'd never done one on his own. I felt like I had worked hard to succeed in my business and to help bring him home from his job. The last thing I was going to have was him hanging around the house thinking, I'm a stay-at-home dad. I was thinking, We're equal partners and we're going to be equal in everything.

To me, that meant sharing the workload of our business, the workload of our kids, and the workload of our laundry. No longer would I bear all the responsibility of getting the kids ready and cooking the food and being perfect and doing this business.

We're still working on it…

When he came home for good from his job, I was already thinking, What's the best way to get him started?

Give him no warning!

I knew Corbin would read the flip chart at that point because he didn't have a choice. If he didn't, then he would have to go back to work. And I knew he was excited about the position he was in—he wanted to learn! I knew a tasting was a perfect opportunity for him to get involved.

After he flipped the chart that morning, women found me and said, "He was so bad." But you know what? He was so bad, he gave them confidence to throw their own tasting parties.

And Corbin had the last laugh: seven women signed up in our business that day.

Two are better than one

If your business is already up and running and then your spouse decides to help you, remember one key thing: Don't criticize. Let them work at their own pace and say what they want to say to customers according to their own personality. If it just kills you to listen, walk out of the room.

That day when I started listening in on Corbin's first tasting, I thought, That's not right, that's not right, that's not right.

After that, I listened to him talk at several tastings, and each time, I thought, That's not how I say it, but if I pick him apart, I'm going to throw him right out of the business.

After a while, I learned to walk away where I couldn't hear him. *Outside.* What I didn't know wouldn't hurt me.

I taught my team of women to celebrate what their husbands did well. I said, "If all he does is look great in the shirt he wears, or if his eyes or smile look beautiful, tell him. Don't criticize a word he says or he'll never get up there again. Tell him you're proud he did it!"

Katie: "When my husband started doing the meetings I was always trying to give him constructive criticism, sometimes in midsentence. Holly told me to say two words: 'Good job!' Then smile and shut up; don't criticize, don't interrupt, and don't ever say how it could be done better.

"That's basically what Holly did for all of us. She was our cheer-leader. It didn't matter how bad we were; she always told us we did a great job! In time, everyone became better at what they were doing and found their own style of presentation. My style was my story."

Confidence is finding your passion and learning to excel at it.

Growing in Confidence
{ CHAPTER 8 }

After quitting his job, Corbin told me his new goal: "Holly, when we reach a certain income level, the first thing I want to do is bring your mom home."

At Corbin's job, my mom was his inside sales person. They got along and had a great working relationship. He wanted to hire her away from a full-time office environment.

Now how many guys would be more worried about bringing their mother-in-law home from the office than keeping their money to spend on themselves?

My mom had worked full time since she was eighteen years old, including the years she raised her three children—my sister, my brother, and me. She missed out on being home with her own three kids, but our goal was to bring her home so she could enjoy her grandchildren.

Because of the business, within six months of Corbin leaving his job, we were able to call her and offer her the ability to leave her full-time office job and work for us and my sister's family while getting to go on field trips, eat lunch, and enjoy activities with her grandkids—things she never ever got to do as a mother. She keeps

our books, reserves hotels, and signs contracts for our business meetings. When we travel to our meetings, our kids love to spend time with her as she takes them to ball practices and movies.

Even though she does a lot for us, in an interview, my mother remarked, "Thank God, I don't have to work!"

I'm sure her comment stems from enjoying her grandchildren and from being a hard worker from the moment she was married. As newlyweds, my parents lived in the college town of Jamestown, North Dakota, where my dad was getting his degree while on a football scholarship. My mom got a job at the state mental hospital working for a psychologist in the alcohol and drug division to pay for their living expenses.

When I was old enough to go to daycare, my mother brought me with her to the daycare center the hospital provided to their employees. Looking back, she doesn't think it was fair to me that I was in there with twenty-six other children. Fair or not, I learned to love being around people.

My mother, Connie, recalls: As a child, she never played with dolls or sat and played alone. She was always out on her bike in the neighborhood. She was always sociable."

Growing up fearless

For my whole life, I've never been afraid to try something new.

Where did that trait come from? Most likely from living in six different states in six years from the ages of nine to fourteen.

My parents divorced when I was nine years old and my sister was four. After that, Carrie and I lived with our mom, whose job transferred us five times from Iowa to North Dakota, Montana, Arkansas, Texas, and finally Oklahoma.

When my mom told me she was getting a divorce, I was devastated because I loved my dad. I also had tons of friends, and I had auditioned for a play and made the lead role of Dorothy in *The Wizard of Oz*. Just when I got the part, I had to move. All of these factors made my first moving experience at nine very hard.

To counteract my sadness, my mom purposely made the move sound fun by saying, "We're moving back to North Dakota where all of your grandparents, aunts, and uncles live!" She did a good job of getting me excited about it. Even so, the first few months I cried almost every day. My dad told me, "Tell the teacher if you need me, and she'll let you call me." I remember calling him, and taking some time to adjust.

Forced to meet new people, I met them by walking right up and saying, "Hi, I'm Holly. I just moved here." I never hid behind my mom's skirt, so to speak.

My mom, sister, and I during our adventure years of moving around.

When we moved to Montana a few years later, I was twelve years old and in seventh grade—a very hard time to leave and make new friends. I internalized my mom's outlook about moving: this is exciting, this is where I'll meet new people, and my mom and sister and I—just us girls!—are going off together on an adventure. It turned out, I made a lot of new friends and I loved skiing the Montana mountains!

After only a year there, I was sad when we had to move. We packed up and moved to Arkansas for my eighth-grade year of school.

During those middle-school years, I would meet people by looking for the biggest group of friends I could find. The biggest group didn't have to be the most popular; it just had to be the biggest circle of friends. I would connect with one person in the group who shared something in common with me. That person would always introduce me to the others.

I had to be outgoing since I didn't have a choice; but that's how I learned to build relationships. To fit in, I had to find out what interested people and get them to talk about themselves rather than focus on myself.

Holly {WOULD}
Focus on you, not on herself.

Even as adults, do any of us have a choice? We have to put ourselves outside of our comfort zones or we'll never have friends and never feel great about ourselves relationally. Still today, I always put myself out there to meet new people.

In my industry, I always tell people, "To meet new people and build your business, go to each group that you are a part of and look for the most sociable person there, the person whose ideas everybody else follows. The most sociable person you can find is going to introduce you to everybody else in the group."

To this day, meeting new people and hearing their unique stories add excitement to my life. My attitude isn't, Hey, can I get you into business with me? Instead, my focus is, I want to hear your story.

When I meet new people I ask them, "Why are you here, where are you from, and what do you do?" And I sincerely love finding out!

Under the influence

They say that opposites attract, and my parents were no exception. My dad was super confident and my mom was a very conservative person who balanced him out by putting on the brakes. My dad saw his limits as higher than the sky; my mom gazed below to measure the fall. Although not necessarily a risk taker, my dad was always excited, always thinking big, always dreaming. On the contrary, my mom believed in security first.

Due to both influences, I balanced somewhere in between. I was a responsible person who didn't cross the line too much, yet I was always driven; I knew what I wanted and I was going to go for it.

Since my sister and I are five years apart in age, we are closer now as adults than we were in childhood. Growing up, she was in elementary school when I was in middle school. When she was in middle school, I thought I was too cool for her because I was in high school. When she was in high school, I was in college and we

both thought we were too cool for each other. But at the same time, we were really tight in certain instances, such as when we spent time together alone.

When we were young, after school we would come home and stay together until our mom got home from work. We would sit down in our apartment and get all of our homework done. Although we lived on a tight budget and didn't have all the new belongings other kids owned, our mom always found us neat apartments to live in.

Across the street from our condo in North Dakota was a gas station with a convenience store. When our mom was running late, we would easily walk to it and buy ravioli or a frozen pizza. We would cook it in one of the store's appliances, and then we would walk back home and eat it for dinner.

To visit our dad, my sister and I would fly by ourselves from North Dakota to Iowa and then later from Montana to Iowa, always connecting in Minneapolis. No one escorted us from gate to gate during our layovers, but I knew I could ask any airline employee wearing a tag to help us if we needed it. My mom was very nice to always give us money for the Fannie Farmer store that was located between our gates. Carrie would buy the chocolate crayons and I would buy the gummy bears. Sometimes we would choose caramel popcorn.

From taking care of my sister starting when I was nine, I learned to be responsible. My mother likes to recall how, at fifteen, I liked to help a ten-year-old girl whose mother had died. I knew she had three brothers but no sister, so I would take her to the mall to go shopping with me.

Learning to take others under my wing built my confidence and set me up for success in business and in life.

Cowboy country

After eighth grade, we moved from Arkansas to Texas where my mom married a man she had met earlier through work. We spent the first half of my ninth-grade year in San Antonio before the contracting company transferred my mother and stepfather to Tulsa, Oklahoma.

Moving can be traumatic and moving to Oklahoma was one of the hardest moves of all. When I entered Union High School in Tulsa, I stepped into a school where most of the kids had been together since the age of four. At fourteen, that was the hardest place for me to meet and make friends.

I had always wanted to be a cheerleader and a member of the drill team, but my family had always moved right before cheer-leading or drill team tryouts so I never had the chance to learn the skills. The cheerleading team at Union was a national championship team, and many of its members had cheered together for many years. When I tried out, I was so nervous that I messed up during my individual routine. I didn't make the team, and that was hard to accept.

I would have loved to have been on the cheer squad or drill team, especially since my closest friends were on those teams. Even though I was embarrassed, I still tried every year to make one of those teams. I kept thinking, Well, I'll keep working at it and I'll keep trying out.

Holly {WOULD}

Keep trying through the embarrassment.

Although I kept trying out, I never made the teams, and each time I would feel sad and upset for a while. Fortunately, I was friends with some girls who weren't on the cheer or drill teams, which helped divert my thoughts of disappointment.

Through all of these up-and-down experiences at various schools, I was learning some valuable lessons that would pay off big-time later on.

It also helped that at fourteen I found a different activity to enjoy. I found retail!

Finding My Future

{ C H A P T E R   9 }

When I filled out an application in a mall clothing store, I hoped they wouldn't notice my age.

A person had to be fifteen to get a job, and I was fourteen and a half. I wanted my own spending money, so I was very happy when the store hired me. By the time they realized their mistake, I had become their number-one sales person. My coworkers hated working shifts with me because I would outsell them all, every time.

How did I do it? Through relationships. I built friendships with the customers by caring enough about their clothing needs to ask questions and show them how to put different combinations together. While they tried on clothes inside the dressing room, I would search for more outside. Consequently, they would enter the store and look for me. When my store threw a sales contest, I won it. I was the best salesperson, hands down.

Holly {WOULD}
Build relationships everywhere.

My passion for sales stemmed from my passion to meet people. I loved helping people feel good about themselves, so in retail, I loved putting customers' clothes together in a way that made them feel proud. When they tried something on, I was honest about telling them which apparel looked best. When they exited my store carrying their purchases and smiling, I felt great satisfaction from knowing they felt better leaving than entering.

That's how I still am today. That's what this whole community commerce industry is about, and that's why I love it!

My father influenced me to care about people. He wouldn't be a superintendent of schools where he lives up in Minnesota if he didn't care about parents and kids. He's a hard worker who always has a smile on his face. He makes people feel better, and I like that about him!

To this day, my dad and I love to watch people and imagine what they're going through. We'll look at two people in a restaurant, for example, and ask each other, What do you think their conversation is about? Tell me their story.

My dad initiated that game. It doesn't matter if he's right or wrong about a person because he truly believes a hundred percent that he knows what that person is going through right now, even a perfect stranger. That's my dad! We have fun together that way.

That observation game of his taught me a valuable business lesson: to be aware of my customers' needs, and consequently, to be willing and open to change.

My mother says her first indication that "this girl could sell anything" was when I was in second or third grade as a Girl Scout Brownie. On my own, I went out in our neighborhood and sold Girl Scout cookies. My mother was hoping I wouldn't get a lot of orders so we wouldn't have to deliver many later on. When it was time to pick up my orders, my mother wasn't too happy when we had to load a carful of cookies into our bronze Chevrolet station wagon, match them to all the customers, and then take hours to deliver them. I had inconvenienced my mother, but I was grateful she helped me.

Knowing the sky is their limit, I want my children to think outside the box, give 110 percent, and set the example for others. Even if it isn't always convenient for me, we will make it happen together.

Senior high

When I was fifteen and a sophomore in high school, my brother Bret was born. When I found out my mother was pregnant with him, I was so embarrassed! When my friends came over to our home, I would say, "Mom! You need to hide!"

Carrie and I had a lot of fun playing with him when he was young, and he is a wonderful uncle to my sons today!

I worked in retail up until the summer of my senior year in high school and then I started working at a women's health club. I liked health and fitness and I liked to exercise, so I took training classes to learn how to teach aerobics. I was the top salesperson in memberships at the Tulsa office, so I was promoted to a manager during my senior year of high school. They sent me to open their office in Muskogee, Oklahoma. Since I took classes only until noon each day, I was able to drive to Muskogee every afternoon to hire and train all the employees. I taught them how to teach aerobics classes, how to sell memberships, how to work behind the front desk, and how to answer phone calls. As soon as I graduated from high school, they flew me to Louisville, Kentucky, for one month to open a fitness center. At seventeen, I lived there in a hotel, hiring and training people.

I look back now and think, I could never let my child do that. My mother says she wouldn't let me do that now either.

They had confidence in me because I was always the best salesperson, and I was the best salesperson because I was passionate about my job! When women came in to buy memberships, I loved to sell them on the benefits. We'd run a lot of promotions where we would call former members and try to get them to join again: "For ninety-nine dollars, you can renew your membership!" I loved the relational part of it, but I liked the thrill of the sale even more.

My business is different. Although I love the excitement of signing someone up, what's even more rewarding is seeing my team succeed. I'm thrilled the most when a person who has struggled finally enrolls somebody. I'm so happy for them!

To succeed in any business, you have to believe in it, be passionate about it, and willing to make sacrifices. You have to be a confident person.

Good sales skills are not what I look for in people. My industry is not about selling. I could have the best salespeople on planet Earth on my team, but if they approach people in a pushy way, people are not going to join. If you don't believe in what you have, you're just trying to sell someone. This business is a sharing industry, so you have to be good at sharing, not at selling.

Holly {WOULD}
Share the benefits.

I always knew I would go to college. My mom encouraged me to get good grades, and although she didn't push me to attend college, I knew she wanted more for me than she experienced. She gave birth to me at eighteen, so she never got to go.

I wanted to go to Oklahoma State University which was funny because all my close high school friends were going to the University of Oklahoma. I felt like OSU was a better fit for me because I really liked the students I had already met from there and I wanted to study marketing. At the time, the OSU business school was ranked one of the top in the nation.

At first, my mom wanted me to go to Tulsa Community College because she thought I should prove myself at a junior college first, but I wanted to go to a big school right away. I heard the university was hosting a Parent Day and I took the initiative to call OSU to find out the date. I suggested to my mom, "Maybe I'll attend OSU after attending TCC for two years, so we should attend the parents' event now at OSU just to see what it's all about." Then I drove her there.

Holly{WOULD}
Take action.

When my mom stepped onto the big campus and experienced the celebration of students and parents and the excitement in the air, she said, "I want this for you. I never got to do this, and this is what you need."

After we went, she never looked back. Of course I had to maintain certain grades, but I knew I would get it done.

If my mom had never felt and seen OSU, I might not have been able to attend there. Environment is important. In your business, if

you will provide a great environment for your customers, they will want to return.

I graduated from high school in 1988. I had saved the wages I earned from age fourteen to eighteen, so when I started college I already had some spending money for clothing and gas money for my car. My mother paid for all of my college tuition plus room and board, and in exchange, I worked during college so I could continue to have my own spending money. Since I enjoyed having my own spending money, I didn't mind working. I taught aerobics for two different employers. Because of all my previous aerobics training, the jobs were easy for me, and I enjoyed them so much, teaching didn't feel like work.

Looking back over my growing-up years, I realize I worked all the time, either taking care of my sister or as an employee. And you know what I think? I'm thankful for my mother's part in pushing me to be responsible because now I can stand on my own two feet.

My mother has done an amazing job raising us three kids. On top of working full time as her electrical contracting employer's first female office manager and transferring every time the company needed her to set up and run a new office, my mother raised my sister and me as a single parent living away from the helpful reach of extended family. Now Bret has graduated from OSU with an engineering degree and is an engineer in Tulsa. My mother will never have to worry about supporting any of us.

Having dinner for my fortieth birthday with Bret, my mom, and Carrie at the Redrock Canyon Grill in Tulsa, July 21, 2010.

College and Corbin

I had a horrible sorority rush. I got cut by everybody.

As soon as I realized I wasn't going to get into one of the most popular sororities, I started talking to friendly girls who were going through rush. "Hey, let's all pledge together. Just think what our pledge class will be like!"

Confidence is turning your loss into a positive.

In the end, our class was full of girls who were so friendly and fun that other girls said they made a mistake and wished they were in ours.

Life is not about the big name; it's about the group of people.

Holly{WOULD}

Build a group of great people.

My sophomore year, I was our sorority's pledge director. I taught the brand-new freshmen the importance of studying, how to manage their schedules, and how to be on their own without their parents. I was like their mother for the year; I was someone they could come to when they didn't have their own mom right there.

My junior year, I was our social director. I loved getting involved in creative activities like setting up parties with the fraternities and sororities. I built relationships with the social directors of the best fraternities to make sure we had the best parties.

Holly{WOULD}
Pursue her passion.

My senior year, I was a sorority rush counselor. I lived in the dorms with the girls as they were going through rush. Going through rush means going through serious issues—girls are getting let go by sororities and getting talked about. Rush is brutal because you find out who your friends are and because you hear a lot of gossip and false rumors people have started about you.

There will always be jealousy, no matter the social circle. We can sit and cry and whine and never go anywhere or just realize that people who see us in a negative light are not our true friends. Therefore, they are not the group of people we need to be around.

Back then, I loved meeting the new girls and building their confidence, and doing so set me up for the business I'm in now.

After four years in college, I got my degree in marketing in 1992, but not before I found Corbin.

Who is this guy?

"Dan, will you introduce me to that guy you're standing next to? He's hot!"

Dan: "I went to high school and college with Corbin, and overall, we were best friends. I had to work my way through college, so I was a houseboy in my fraternity, which meant I cooked. Holly was in a sorority and that's how I met her. She was a very impressive young lady, supersweet, so when Holly asked me to introduce them to each other, I said, 'Absolutely!'"

As Dan introduced us, I knew I had heard Corbin's name before. "You're Corbin Roush? Oh! I don't like you."

"What!"

"I've never met you, but I've heard you're always in the wrong place at the wrong time, catching the blame for most of the bad things that happen in college."

Two years older than me, Corbin had already graduated from OSU. I was about to enter my senior year of college at the end of that summer.

What I didn't know at the time was that Corbin has the biggest heart. He got blamed for everything because he came across as a tough guy, which he wasn't at all. He was a big teddy bear softy guy.

I thought Corbin was good-looking, so we started dancing. I could tell he was a good person with great morals and values who just needed the right person to bring them out. He asked for my phone number, and we started dating.

After college, Corbin was hired at Walmart Corporate. Part of their policy was that he work in a store for up to two years. They sent him out to a small Texas town in the middle of nowhere.

Miserable, he decided to come home to Tulsa and I met him his first night back.

I liked what I saw, but I didn't like that he didn't have a job. I was a go-getter who was going to marry someone with dreams, goals, and a great career. After I got to know him, I found out he had a degree in marketing and he was looking for the right job in that field. If he hadn't left Texas that night, we might not have met.

I was looking for someone who didn't mind working hard and who was a family man. Family was important to me, and I could see a strong family value in Corbin right away because I observed how close his family was and how they took care of each other.

He was raised in a strong Christian home. My family attended church some Sundays and on all the important holiday weekends. I remember going to a class when I was in ninth grade. The minister kept asking me questions that I thought were inappropriate because they were very personal.

When I walked out of there, I told my mom, "I'm done."

She said, "When you're old enough, you can choose the church you want to attend."

From ninth grade on, I knew I would choose something different. That church wasn't a fit for me, and I was bored, but somehow, I always knew that I wanted to marry somebody who would go to church with me and our kids. It wasn't as much about which church we attended as it was about going to church every week as a family.

Broken bones and mended hearts

Dan: "Corbin was one heck of an athlete. As a freshman at the largest high school in Oklahoma, they were looking at putting him up at quarterback. Not only was he a phenomenal athlete, but he was always very smart too, with a 3.6 GPA. Corbin and I ran several marathons together. He did a great job. He knows how to come up with a game plan and stick to it. He's a finisher."

In the middle of a football game his junior year, Corbin's ankle broke. He kept waiting for his dad to come down out of the bleachers to take him to the hospital. Suddenly, his uncle came down and told him, "Corbin, your dad has suffered a massive heart attack and he isn't going to make it. He's at the hospital."

Shocked, Corbin wanted to see his dad right away—forget about his ankle! He went to the hospital, but not in time. He never got to see his dad, his best friend.

At the time, the local newspaper told the story and my mom read it. When I started dating Corbin, she said, "I remember that name!" It's amazing how life can be one giant circle of experiences.

Corbin heading to quarterback a game in Broken Arrow his junior year, fall of 1985.

We dated and then broke up for a little bit, but we couldn't deny it. Our hearts said we were right for each other. We were married on July 10, 1993.

What to Do, What to Do...

{ C H A P T E R   1 0 }

After college, I worked for eight years in two different careers. During those years, I gave birth to our first two sons and returned to work both times. My first job was at Stokely Outdoor Advertising and my second was at Holland Hall, Tulsa's prestigious preparatory school, as Director of Alumni Relations in the marketing department. When the famous British primatologist, Jane Goodall, came to Tulsa and visited Holland Hall, I enjoyed the privilege of helping advertise her appearance. I remember her story landing on TV stations and in *USA Today*. Then after that, my third job was in pharmaceutical sales.

Corbin wanted me to stay home with our sons. He tried to talk me into it, beg me into it. But I had never aspired to the life of a stay-at-home mom. I had always pictured myself as a corporate career woman, rising to the top and running a company. For me, making a decision to stay home was hard!

There came a day when the decision was no longer difficult. At a pharmaceutical conference in California, all of a sudden my eyes were opened to things I hadn't noticed in four years—partying, drinking a ton, and some infidelity. I realized it had always

happened right under my nose, but I had been oblivious to it. I thought, This is not a good situation for me to be around.

In a defining moment, I knew I had to walk away. I picked up the phone and called Corbin.

"I'm ready," I said.

After I decided to stay home with my children who were four-and-a half and one, I quickly realized that my new full-time role as a mom was harder for me than being out there in the workforce. Even though I loved being a mom, I was no longer receiving a pat on the back for work well done. I missed the sense of accomplishment, something I think most moms miss who have worked outside their homes. I still cherished the goals, the details, and the adult interaction of the corporate world. I felt like I was no longer contributing to the world at large, and that I had lost a piece of my independence.

Poor Corbin! When he would walk in the door, tired from a long day at the office, I would fire questions at him: "What did you do today? How many sales did you make?" On and on, I would try to force him to relive his day. He needed a break from it, while I needed to live vicariously through his job. I missed the work world, but I had dedicated myself to my family.

Finding the time

Since many families today have their backs pinned against the wall financially, I think lots of stay-at-home moms know they need to get a job but are worried about neglecting their families.

Often, they know their resumes are so outdated that they aren't qualified for anything substantial out in the job market. Yet, some moms aren't able to get an entry-level job because they're overqualified. Most moms want to be home for the sake of their children, and since they already have a million things their husbands and kids rely on them to do, they're afraid to get out in the workforce. They know their husbands are stressed-out from carrying the family financial burden alone in an increasingly downward-spiraling economy, but they aren't sure how to help.

How can a stay-at-home mom feel comfortable dedicating time to a business? How can she find the time without neglecting her current responsibilities?

Something I love about being in your own business is that it can be as small or as large as a family wants it to be. Stay-at-home moms can help their children and spouses by contributing a little bit of time every day, time that can produce something big for their own families, as well as for others in their world. My friend, Maranda, found this to be true.

Maranda's story, in her words

I met Holly and Corbin for the first time when my husband, Dan, and I were dating. Their first son, Dakota, was a newborn. Every time we traveled to Tulsa we would stop by to see them, and they came to our wedding.

Holly got me my first job in pharmaceuticals. She called her district manager and said, "Maranda is a person you should talk to."

Since I had come from a nursing background, I was clueless and insecure. I was in Oklahoma City and she was in Tulsa, but we talked almost every day. She was my mentor.

I would call her and say, "What do I do about this?"

Always wise and upbeat, she always had specific, direct answers that helped me. "This is how you do it. This is what I've done."

She was always so completely confident that she left no room for doubt in my mind about doing what she advised.

We moved to Dallas where Dan was flying for American Airlines, and I changed jobs. Holly and I hadn't talked in maybe two to four months when she called me one day, almost hyperventilating.

"Maranda, it's big, it's really big!"

I thought, Did I win the lottery?

"There's this ah-key berry."

That sounds disgusting!

"Oprah's talking about it, and I've been reading all this stuff on it, and it helps joints!"

Okay, now you have my attention!

Nine months after my son was born, I had reconstructive surgery on my hip. I anticipated a six-week recovery, but six months later, I was still walking with a cane. I received hip injections, but was told, "We don't know what else to do for you."

Since the pharmaceutical company I worked for wouldn't allow me to use a cane, I had to limp everywhere without it.

When Holly called me, she was thinking she had something to help me. "I don't know anything about it, but I've been reading and you've got to try it! Do you want it wholesale or retail?"

Notice, she didn't say, "I don't know if you're interested in this."

Holly{WOULD}
Expect a yes.

"I'll get it wholesale!" I said. She was so excited about it, she got me fired up, too! What did I have to lose?

"Give me your social-security and credit-card information."

I didn't know why she needed those personal pieces of information, but I gave them to her. I trusted my friend.

When I joined that day, I didn't know there was a business opportunity. After America's 9/11 tragedy, Dan's pay got cut by 48 percent. Right before Holly's phone call, things had become really tight.

Those first cases of juice showed up looking like moonshine—sometimes the bottles were clear, sometimes colored, sometimes the labels were upside down—but I thought, Holly said this will work!

The juice was a luxury item for us, and because we didn't know about its financial opportunity, we stopped receiving automatic shipments of it.

Holly's response? "It's okay," and she kept right on going, telling more people about it.

At Dan and Corbin's high school reunion, Corbin told Dan how much money he and Holly were making—twelve thousand dollars a week! Then he said, "This is not a traditional business—you can do it in five minutes here and ten minutes there. Just go with it through consistent, positive action toward your goal. This is a part-time business with a full-time income. When are you going to do this, Dan?"

We thought, Oh my gosh! We have some friends who are making crazy money, and here we are all maxed-out and stressed-out! They have the lifestyle we want—if they can do it, we can do it!

I got back on the juice. The change in my hip was gradual, and Dan noticed it first.

"Maranda, why aren't you complaining so much about your hip?"

When I had stopped using a cane to keep my pharmaceutical job, according to Dan, I "raised cane." I was in so much pain! I was so miserable riding in the car that we couldn't drive to Tulsa anymore to see our family.

Dan suspected that the juice was alleviating my pain, so I decided to test it. I stopped drinking it for a few days, and when I did, I felt terrible! I then knew it was the juice that was helping me and I went back on it.

At the time, we had started multiple streams of income for our family: Dan was working seventy hours a week in his own shutter/blind business, we were raising exotic deer, and I was still selling pharmaceuticals. Our two sons were three months old and three years old.

The opportunity fits

Maranda continues:

I called Holly and asked, "How can I find time for this business?"

"You don't need to find time. Just integrate it into your day. At lunch every day, if you're not talking to doctors, talk to someone about the juice. But talk to two people a day. When can you make two phone calls a day?"

"I can make two phone calls at night."

"Make your contact list and make two phone calls a night."

I started signing up people, and Holly provided me with a binder of information. She had researched and put together binders just like the ones we presented to doctors in pharmaceutical sales. The pages included the results of Holly's research such as product facts, testimonials, goal-setting information, and everything she was personally doing to build her business. She had to duplicate herself this way because her business was growing fast! I would go to Kinkos to make copies to give to new people I enrolled.

Today, we are Hawaiian Blue Diamond Executives, and women are always asking me, "Why do you wear really tall high heels when you're already five-foot-nine?"

I'm happy to respond, "Because for two-and-a-half years, I had to wear unattractive flats. I could hardly lift my leg and I moved my feet funny because I lost my muscle strength. Holly got me back in high heels."

And that's not all.

After four years on the juice, I was able to go off my asthma inhaler. I don't even get a prescription for it anymore.

Laura's reason

Instead of worrying about neglecting your children, let them be your reason to achieve your family's dreams.

Holly {WOULD}
See her children as a reason,
not as an excuse.

That's what Laura did, starting when her sons were four and nine. This is her story, in her words:

My son, Brennan, has Down Syndrome, yet I went Blue Diamond in ten months with Brennan in school just a few hours at a time, three days a week.

At first I wondered how I would build a successful business while taking care of him. My husband came up with a great strategy when he said, "Get up early."

So I set my alarm for 4:30 a.m. I had to prioritize my time.

I would get up early before my family to get myself in the mindset of a successful day. I would have my quiet time, and I would decide which two or three new people to contact and which people to follow up with. I would study online so I could answer people's questions. Our upline teammates all lived in Florida, so new people weren't calling them, they were calling us! We had to have the answers. So I had a couple of hours to study in the mornings before I got Luke off to his school and Brennan off to his.

As my business picked up, I cut tennis back from three to four days a week to one. But I wanted to! It was so much fun that it didn't feel like I was sacrificing at all. I told my husband that I had two whys for reaching a goal of one thousand dollars a week, and both involved hiring people: (1) a housekeeper, and (2) some help for Brennan. When I reached that financial goal, I was able to hire a sitter in the summer for Brennan, and that's what freed me to go Diamond and Blue Diamond.

I never used Brennan as an excuse not to build this business. Instead, he has always been my biggest why. He will never be able to leave our house, so this business is a way to secure residual income for his financial future without any financial burden falling on our son, Luke.

Aside from the financial benefits, the physical benefits of providing the best nutrition for him fulfilled a big why for us. Lots of special-needs kids have weaker immune systems, and like Brennan, have more trouble eating a good variety of foods than other kids. This juice that is the equivalent of thirteen servings of fruits is great nutrition for him.

Every day, I'm so grateful for the physical and financial benefits of this business.

Finding help

Another thing I think stay-at-home moms wonder is, Who will take care of my children if I add business meetings to my schedule?

To help out with your children, make it a priority to find sitters you love and trust. We are grateful for our family members and sitters our kids love.

At a local Christian college, I walked on campus and put fliers on bulletin boards in the education department, the nursing department, and the dorms. Several girls called. I invited them over to our home where I asked a few questions and collected a few references that I contacted.

All I had to do was find one or two great ones and they led me to more like themselves. Just before one of them moved, I asked her, "Hey, will you give me some backups? Who do you know that would be a good fit with my kids?"

The answers are all found in the network!

It's important to find sitters you feel very comfortable leaving your kids with, fun people they're excited to see. We found a couple of babysitters our kids absolutely love, so when we walk out the door they simply and calmly say, "Bye!" If you have a babysitter your kids can't stand, you'll feel guilty leaving them. We make the experience fun for them by saying, "So-and-so's coming! You're going to have fun!"

We have a babysitter named Emily who actually lives in another town, but she is willing to drive 106 miles to stay with our kids. We trust her very much and our kids love her. When our kids see us walking out the door, they're fine because they know she'll take care of them. She takes them to cooler places than we do!

When you leave your house, isn't it nice to know that someone cares about your kids enough to make sure they are totally fine? Finding this kind of babysitter frees you to work efficiently and effectively.

Charlie's advice

When I first started in the business, I was waiting till Corbin fell asleep to prepare for the next day. I would take care of business details such as sending my e-mails and making the boys' lunches until two or three in the morning.

It was hard.

I asked Charlie and Debbie, "What do I do to help my kids adjust to my new business? For the last few years, they've seen me home all the time. To keep everyone happy, I'm working really late once they all fall asleep. I'm exhausted when I get up and some days they see me walk out the door when they're used to seeing me home every minute. I'm unsure about what to do. Can you help me? Have you seen this in other families?"

Charlie answered, "Holly, get your kids involved. Sit down with them, dream with them, and write down their goals. That way they'll know, when their family hits a certain business level, they'll get to do a certain exciting thing. So rather than grabbing your ankles when you're walking out the door, they're cheering you on."

Charlie was right. By taking his advice, all of a sudden I was coming home to excited kids, who would routinely ask, "How many people were there? How many guests? Did they sign up?"

Holly {WOULD}
Include her children.

Have you ever sat down with your family to see what they're dreaming about? It's incredible!

After you listen to your children's dreams, set big and small goals with corresponding rewards. Your conversation might go something like this: "When we go Bronze, you can get new pairs of shoes. When we go Gold, let's go to your favorite restaurant. When we go Ruby, we'll take you on a trip with us."

Later on when Corbin joined me in the business, Dakota saw Corbin and me home one night and said, "Why are you home? You need to go! Go to a meeting! We're fine!"

That's what you want from your kids!

Help from Heidi

The first day I met Heidi was before I actually signed up in the business, and she was the first person I told about the juice. We were working out side by side on treadmills. She had just moved to Tulsa from Kansas City.

I said, "How do you like Tulsa?"

She said, "It's nice, but I would rather be in Kansas City."

Here is the rest of the story in Heidi's words:

Holly hadn't tasted the juice yet, she hadn't even signed up, but she was all excited. I was the first one to pour ice-cold water on her, I'm sure. I said to her, "No thanks, but you should do it." That's the polite way to say, "No, heck no." I doubted it would be a good product, I wasn't interested, and I definitely didn't want to do it as a business.

Holly didn't mind.

I said to her, "Hey listen, when your juice comes in, bring me a bottle. I will be happy to taste it." That bottle sat in the refrigerator for months before I eventually poured it down the drain.

I watched Holly for nine months. She really got my attention when I started hearing rumors, not only of good health, but of how much money she and so many of our mutual friends were making in this business. I casually mentioned it to my husband and he said, "Now why aren't we doing this?"

Ugh! Great!

He said, "Do you think we should at least go and find out what it is we're saying no to?"

We got a sitter and we went to our first tasting party. We listened to Holly tell about the nutrition in the juice. Hearing that, I was in immediately! I knew we needed to be drinking it. And then she started talking about the business. My husband is a business-man so he just saw it!

Steve and Heidi

I was kind of dreading the business part. I just wanted to drink it. I didn't want to work it, and here's why: *I thought I was really busy!*

I was a stay-at-home mom with two kids and I was having a great time. Steve was providing very well for us through his job in the oil and gas business. My days were always busy. I had a workout and then sometimes I had lunch out with friends. When somebody had a baby, I made dinner and took it over. I volunteered at church in the nursery and at school once a week making copies and some-times cutting things out. That was my very important schedule, and I felt like I was doing great things for people!

I liked the thought that maybe we could make some money at this, but I wasn't sure if I could do it. I was so afraid of failing that I wouldn't even allow myself to try.

The light came on when my husband, Steve, said, "You know what, Heidi? I realize we've got enough money coming in, but I wouldn't mind a little help."

I was mortified.

That was all it took for me to have a whole new attitude. I had always wanted to serve. Now I realized I could have a much bigger impact if I dug in and got a hold of a vehicle like this business. I could help people with their health and maybe their finances too—all the while contributing to our family's bottom line. That's a lot more than I could do with a pair of scissors and some tape.

I was able to look at this and say, "Oh my gosh, this is something Steve and I can do together. We can set a goal and encourage our kids, Mac and Clara, to be a part it."

We discovered that one job even little kids could do was price the business tools, such as brochures and CDs. Using a pricing gun similar to those at retail stores, our kids put price stickers on all the tools we sold at our meetings. That activity usually escalated into pricing the couch, pricing the table, pricing the dog...

My business allowed me to model traits that I wanted to instill in my kids, and they have witnessed a difference in me. Setting personal goals and helping others reach their goals is just a natural by-product of the business. Now my kids are goal-setters, too. They believe in themselves and work hard for what they want to achieve.

Steve said to me, "Listen, I know you would like to go back to Kansas City, but what's our plan? How are we going to do that? If you build this like Holly has, we'll get you back to Kansas City where your family and friends are!"

And that's exactly what happened. We built a residual income that allowed us to move back home. We're right where we want to be, and it's a dream come true! My husband and I became Blue Diamond Executives in the company.

Sacrifice to Success
{ C H A P T E R   1 1 }

About that lake house we lost…

When I first moved to Oklahoma at fourteen, I noticed that a lot of residents owned lake houses. I grumbled, "They're all rich people I don't know, so I'll never get to go!" I wanted to have a lake house someday.

Years later, I had my eye on a community of thirty-five lake homes where my sister had a second home by the water. The layers of houses in that neighborhood started with the most expensive ones near the lake, and then extended on back, with some less expensive houses by the pool. Every time we drove into that community, a certain house caught my eye.

Sitting on a corner overlooking the entire lake, the house had a huge wraparound porch and was painted in periwinkle blue and yellow. To me, it was the neatest one in the whole neighborhood. Even though I loved it, the owners had lived there since it was built so I thought there was no way they were going to leave.

The houses by the pool were fine, and since buying one would get us into that neighborhood, Corbin and I chose a house by the pool. At 4:00 p.m. the day before our 8:00 a.m. closing, Corbin had

to call and tell me to cancel everything! I had to move fast! I called the mortgage company and the boat deliveryman and said, "My husband just lost two-thirds of his income. Sorry, but we can't do this." We lost all our deposits on that house.

Corbin was devastated. He felt humiliated asking me to cancel a dream of mine. He was also embarrassed about uninviting friends we'd asked to spend the weekend with us on the lake!

As hard as that experience was, I thought, If we just keep building our business, something better is going to happen for us. God has a bigger plan. This isn't where we're supposed to be.

In March, about seven months after we had to cancel the closing of the house by the pool, the house we loved by the lake went up for sale. By then our juice business had doubled, enabling us to buy that house. Instead of settling for less, we were able to buy the lake house of our dreams!

My goal was to share our house with as many people as possible, so before the summer started, I made a list of every family I wanted to invite to the lake that summer. I loved seeing the children's faces light up! For some families, it was the only vacation they enjoyed all year. My goal was for them to come to the house, relax, and enjoy as we did all the entertaining.

Dakota and his friends sitting on Jet Skis at our lake house on Grand Lake, Memorial Day weekend, 2010.

If it wasn't for this business, owning our dream lake house wouldn't have happened, and it took sacrifice and persistence on our part to achieve it.

All together now

To succeed in business, sacrifices must be made. Corbin and I prioritized our time. We asked ourselves, What's important? What do our kids *have* to have? What do they *have* to do?

If you have sons like ours, you know they want to get involved in every soccer, basketball, baseball, and football team. But guess what happens when they get involved in every single sport?

They have to be there and so do you. You both feel guilty if they miss.

It's almost easier to sit down with your kids and say, "We're going to take this season off to meet a family goal."

Corbin and I made a decision: We're going Imperial, Crowne, and Double Crowne, a decision we know will eventually benefit our family and friends. We decided to involve our sons in the commitment and sacrifice necessary to achieve it.

When we made that decision, we sat down with our sons and said, "Mom and Dad are going to run real hard. You're going to come along for the ride. We're going to see this country together. We're going to meet new people. You guys are going to have the time of your lives!

"But you know what? You're going to have to make a sacrifice. You're going to have to miss baseball this spring. You're not going to be able to play golf this summer. We're not going to be at the lake house that much. We're going on the road!

"But guess what? When we hit Imperial, we're going to let each of you guys pick what you want."

Afterward, we talked to each of our sons individually.

"Dakota, if you could have anything when Mom and Dad go Imperial, what would it be? Anything you want. What is it you want?"

Twelve-year-old Dakota said, "All I want is a yellow Lab."

I thought, Wow! We don't really like dogs. Corbin was thinking, We hate dogs.

But we said, "Okay! That's great!"

Next, we approached Drake, who didn't have any clue what Dakota had just told us.

"Drake, if we go Imperial, what do you want?"

Nine-year-old Drake said, "I'd kill for a black Lab!"

Another Lab!

Then we asked our six-year-old. "All right, Ethan! Anything you want."

"I want to have the biggest, baddest golf cart at the lake house with big knobby tires and my own stereo and I want to be able to drive it anywhere I go!"

It was enlightening to hear what they wanted—their requests were much simpler than I expected. Our sons turned sacrifice into fun!

Spending some family time together at the lake over Thanksgiving, 2009.

Thinking of others

Is your family building something together?

Corbin and I have grown in many ways since we started growing our business together, and our sons have grown right along with us.

So will *your* children when you include them in your business!

On our way to school, our sons like to ask us if people have reached their goals: "Hey, did so-and-so make it to Hawaii? Are they coming with us? Mom, when do you think they're going to get to Hawaiian Blue? When do you think they'll go Black Diamond? When are they going to get their Mercedes?"

They've learned to cheer people on just as much as Corbin and I are cheering people on in their business.

Coaches tell us, "Man, Dakota needs to be a motivational speaker! He's the one getting all the kids fired up! He helps the kids who are down; he's such an encourager."

I teach my kids, when there's a child at lunch by himself, go grab him; when there's a child on the playground who wasn't invited to play, go invite him.

Holly {WOULD}
Expect her family to care about others.

A parent from school approached us and said, "As much as you guys are doing, and I see everything you're doing to help people, I've never seen a set of kids who are so happy. They always have the biggest smiles on their faces."

Are Corbin and I gone sometimes? Do we run? Absolutely! But when we're with our kids, we are *with* them, spending quality time!

One day after a meeting, Dakota said, "Mom! Dad! I get it! I understand why you run so hard. I want you to go!"

I said, "Why?"

"Because I see all the people you are helping."

From our example, I want my kids to learn not to be selfish, sitting on a couch every night in front of the TV. I want them to learn to get out there and help other people's dreams come true.

Emily: "My husband and I do the same thing Corbin and Holly do. If Kevin's on the road, I'm home. If Corbin's on the road, Holly's home. If you look at the scheme of the year, it's maybe five weekends of the year that we're gone together.

"When my husband and I can pick up our kids from school, we can both help them with homework. We can coach their sports. We can do these things in the afternoons, a time when dads typically aren't around. And then, in the evening, when we leave for a tasting at 7:00 p.m., it's that last hour before bedtime when all they are doing is vegging out on the couch anyway and winding down from the day. So we get the quality time with our kids, not just the vegging-out time with them."

Where do you want to be?

Goal-setting is so important, not only for your business but for your family. When you set goals, be specific.

We love teaching our children a goal-setting habit from an early age. Corbin likes to sit down with them and ask them to tell him their goals for their school year. He'll ask, "Where do you want to be in football? What do you want to do in school?"

We know they think about it because Dakota has turned around and asked a friend, "Hey, what's your goal this year? How many points do you want to average in basketball?"

When asked about his current sports and dreams for his athletic future, Dakota said, "I play basketball on my school team and on my tournament team, the Steelers. I'm a guard in basketball and the quarterback on my football team. I would like to go as far as I can in sports, and then afterward, do something like sports broadcasting."

In your business, if you aren't writing down your goals, you're never going to achieve them. What is your goal and when do you want to hit it? Before you assign a date, think about how fast you can work to reach your goal. How much time per week is your family willing and able to commit?

A little bit here and there

I tell people in my business to fit it into the nooks and crannies of their day; they don't have to sacrifice their children or their marriage for it.

Spend quality time with your kids, then use some of that extra time you waste on trivial things to sacrifice for your family. Small sacrifices will take your business to another level.

Think of those five, ten, or fifteen minutes here and there that you normally waste doing something that isn't going to further anybody, and use them to focus on your business.

I was the queen of network television. I knew every show that was on from 8:00-10:00 every night of the week. After our boys went to bed, Corbin and I would sit there and watch those shows.

I decided to walk away from the TV and use that time to build my contact list, listen to a teaching CD, read a motivational book, call somebody, or check in on my team. Instead of wasting time while the kids slept, I was productive.

Holly{WOULD}
Fit business into the nooks and crannies of the day.

Emily: "It's definitely a balance. My priority is my family. My husband and I owned companies when I got started with this. I couldn't walk away from my commitment there. So this business was definitely a side deal. When we started making over ten thousand dollars a week, it was hard to say this business was our side deal because our other businesses never paid us that well. We came to the point where we were four years into it before we sold our companies. Holly and Corbin were full time after a year, so their commitment level could always be a little bit more than ours.

"I've had conversations with people, 'If you want to go Gold, I'm going to give you all the information you need to get there. Take the information and decide if you want to go at a snail's pace or at the speed of a jet plane. Decide your speed for yourself and how to put it into your own life.'"

With your spouse and children, make a time commitment. If you decide to tell people about your business opportunity five times a week, what will that look like for you? Five nights a week? Or one night meeting, two mornings, and two lunches with people? Or three nights a week, one morning, and one lunch? Whatever you decide, stick to it, write it on your calendar, and you will see your business grow.

Along the way to reaching big goals, remember to celebrate small successes. In my industry, we celebrate the woman who now gets out of bed easier and the man who just lost six pounds.

Worth it!

Our business has brought us so many dear friends! No matter your business, you will meet new people. In ours, I've found myself drawn to people who are positive, who want more, and who instill good behavior and good values into their own families. Those friends have become our support system, and that support system means everything!

Through these quality kinds of relationships, I'm connecting my kids to a lot of other kids down the road of life. My sons are building a network without even realizing it.

Across the country, no matter where they go to school, I know they'll have somebody. If they get stuck on the road somewhere, they will have someone to call for help. My kids are actually safer now than before I decided to follow my heart into this business.

With friends from across the country at Lake Lure, North Carolina, to spend Fourth of July week, 2011.

How many young kids can say, "I have friends all across the country"?

Holly {WOULD}
Surround herself with positive people.

In your business, if you'll always follow the road full of people who are positive, excited, and confident, you'll glean those attributes from them over time. I believe you are who you hang around.

Another benefit of a community commerce business such as ours is that our summers together are amazing! We load up our three children and we are gone all summer building this business together as a family.

How many people have the ability to take off for three months with their family, knowing they're getting paid every Friday?

But before we got here, we had to realize we were going to miss out on some things; we had to sacrifice. And look how far it got us!

If you sacrifice and persist in your commitment, your business will grow. You can change your family's entire future!

Who Cares?

I'll never forget our first experience drinking the juice with our sons.

"Hey, kids," Corbin announced, "Mom's got some funky new juice and we're all gonna start drinking it tomorrow."

Drake was so picky he wouldn't even eat a cheeseburger. He said, "I am *not* drinking that juice. No way!"

But since Drake is also our little businessman, Corbin said, "I tell you what! Every morning you drink Momma's funky little juice, we'll give you a dollar."

"Okay, I'll do anything for that!"

When the next morning rolled around, it was time to start drinking our juice. We were ready! Corbin lined up five SpongeBob Dixie cups, took the juice out of the fridge, and started to pour it.

I stopped him. "No, no, no! Shake it! Shake it real good!"

"Shake it! Why?"

"Oh, I heard there are some chunks in the juice right now and you won't want to feel them in your throat."

The look on Corbin's face said, What in the world have you gotten us into?

Drake piped up, "Dad! If chunks are a part of the deal, it's going to cost you *two* dollars!"

Lucky bottles

When customers started asking me about the chunks sliding down their throats, I said, "Hey! They fight for those in Florida where Brig and his friends live! That's the most nutritious part of the drink!" All around Tulsa, we started saying, "Oh, you got the lucky bottle with the chunks!"

One day, a girl called me to say, "I just found a leaf in my bottle!"

I responded, "Oh, you got the lucky bottle! I didn't get a leaf, so may I have it?"

Too many people would have thought, Oh, it's all over! There's a leaf in the bottle!

I thought, Is a leaf really going to hurt someone? No. So I laughed about it with her!

If someone was very negative about a situation, I would say, "Let's trade your case of juice for a case of mine. The juice company has always taken care of us, so I know they'll do the right thing." Then I would call the company and deal with my own case of juice, behind the scenes.

Holly{WOULD}

Turn a negative into a positive.

Thinking positively brings confidence in your product.

One day, Corbin pulled up at a friend's law office to show him the juice. He opened the trunk of his car and then opened a cooler to grab a bottle.

To his surprise, every single label had floated to the top of the ice! He thought, Now what do I do? So he stuck a label back on a bottle and walked into the office.

Someone saw him and said, "Hey, your label fell off!"

We couldn't let negatives like that define our success. We found people who couldn't care less, even though we seemed to be pedaling moonshine in a bottle!

Holly {WOULD}
Keep running hard and having fun!

Today, the product is perfect every time it arrives. Despite its flaws in the beginning, the juice company still went to a billion-dollar business, and it's still growing!

Three strikes, you're out?

When I got started in the business, I had several strikes against me. Thousands of people had already joined ahead of me, giving them what some see as an advantageous position in the company. Furthermore, I had to build both sides of my team from scratch, creating extra work for me from the very beginning. People I loved told me I was crazy to pursue this business.

I wasn't born rich, so I didn't have wealthy prospects to call on. I had never done relational marketing, and had never wanted to do relational marketing, so I was a little embarrassed at the thought of approaching people who might laugh at me. I hadn't seen the product, or even tasted it. Our company didn't supply tools for success as they do now. I had access to a couple of Web sites where I could print information in black and white— not professional looking at all. And, I'm a visual learner, so I could not understand the compensation plan without someone writing it down and drawing it out in person. Since I didn't know anyone in the company in my town, I started alone, with no one to help me.

Did I get discouraged and quit? No, I kept thinking, What if? If I don't jump in now, what if I wish I had a year from now? What if this turns into something big?

I decided I didn't care if someone laughed at me. I thought, You know what? Laugh at me! I don't care because I'm going to laugh later.

And you know what? People who didn't get in with me right away have called me to say, "I thought this would die out after the first month, but it didn't, so I guess it's time for me to get in. By the way, where would I have been if I had gotten in nine months ago when you first told me about it?"

"Oh, about five thousand people up, but that's fine. If you would have gotten in with me nine months ago, you probably wouldn't have gone anywhere because your heart wasn't in it. Now, you're going to do something with it."

And they all are!

Negative words

What do you do when you have a worrier in your family?

When close family members question my decisions, I think, Okay, there might be something to this. I evaluate what they say because sometimes they're right. When they're wrong, I just have to shrug off their words. I realize they probably said what they did because they love me.

Holly {WOULD}
Give people a break.

It's a different story when someone is constantly negative toward me. It reminds me of third grade.

I don't remember much about living in Des Moines, Iowa, but I do remember my white-blonde hair at seven years of age and walking about a mile home after school with my sister. The reason I remember this is because some boys who were probably in seventh grade would dart out from behind trees and throw worms at us because they didn't like my hair. Once they found us each time, I would burst into tears and run the rest of the way home with Carrie by my side.

Now when someone gets me down, the first thing I do is pick up the phone and call someone who lifts me back up. I call the kind of person who is always upbeat, the kind of person who spreads good news.

What I don't do when I call someone is repeat the discouraging words I just heard. Rehearsing them only magnifies the negative situation, and the two of us end up double-telling the story, a story I'm trying to forget. To be honest, I don't even tell Corbin. If I did, he would be mad because he wants to protect me.

I simply choose to think, It is what it is. I'm not going to go back-wards. I can't change what happened and I'm not going to try because it would waste time and energy. I don't have time and energy to waste! Ultimately, I know I'm taking care of my family.

After listening for a while to the excitement in a positive friend's voice, I think, Ah! This is my sane place! Then, I'm able to go back out and work with people again.

To stay confident in your business, go to the place or the person who picks you back up.

As long as you live, you may never fully understand why people think it's okay to speak negatively to you, but you can choose what to do about it. After you're finished crying and letting the words eat at you, and trust me, I know they do, you can sit and listen to that negativity in your head over and over again or you can refuse to believe those negative words!

After negative words have bombarded me, and I've looked to see if they contain any truth I need to adapt to, I refuse to second-guess myself. If I wasted time that way, Corbin and I would stop in our tracks. I'm not going to do that!

I believe in taking charge of our own destinies. The more people nag at me, the more determined and tenacious I become.

Holly {WOULD}
Keep going despite negative words!

Negative spouse

"Holly, my back and knees don't hurt as much!" Corbin said. His body was beat up from running in five marathons. After drinking the juice, he suddenly noticed a change.

After admitting it to me, I said, "Would you please share that at one of my meetings? Please?" At the time, no men had ever showed up.

Corbin said, "All right, I'll come down and talk."

This is what happened, in Corbin's words:

"Holly was so excited! Finally, she had a guy! Soon after our conversation, I was upstairs watching ESPN while one of Holly's meetings was starting downstairs. She bounded up the stairs and said, 'Hey, can you come downstairs and talk now?'

"I walked downstairs to a packed house. Everybody's eyes were glued on me. I could see what they were thinking: 'Oh, he's going to talk! My husband will get involved now. This is going to be big! This is going to be huge!' You'd have thought the Second Coming had just happened.

"I said, 'Hey ladies! I'm fired up about this juice. I have to tell you, I'm proud of you! You're making some money and you're getting your friends to do this with you. This juice has helped me out tremendously. See this hand? I got it shot off! I started drinking the juice, and it grew back!'

"Not one lady laughed. A bunch of fingers pointed me back upstairs, and they weren't index fingers, if you know what I mean.

"'Go to your room!' Holly demanded.

"I slept on the couch for three nights, just for poking a little fun!

"Despite the embarrassment I caused, neither Holly nor her team quit. They kept building their business! Every time I would turn negative on her, she would get up and leave the room. She didn't want to hear it. She always stayed positive and always stayed focused. As a child, Holly had quit her basketball team when a relative yelled, 'You need to hustle! You're embarrassing me,' but now she had grown in confidence and stayed the course."

No's

No matter what business you're in, you're going to get no's and you're going to get people who criticize. But for every one of those, you're going to get someone who says, "That's a great idea!"

People have said to me, "All of *your* friends say yes!"

Are they kidding? I just haven't told them about the no's. I don't get stuck on the no's—ever! I focus on the yeses. I find the ones who believe in me and want to roll up their shirtsleeves and partner with me.

Holly {WOULD}
Never get stuck on the no's.

Instead of worrying about what your friends are going to say, I promise you, if you get out there and help them physically and financially, your friends are going to love what you do!

Don't worry about rejection. If you'll stay excited about improving lives, you'll find the people who want to lock arms with you and run to success. Don't let no's stop you! On a day when someone who you absolutely knew would say yes tells you no, call your positive friend and let her pick you back up. Then go ask another friend.

Getting back up and doing something again makes you confident.

If you shut down right away, you'll kill your dream. Are a handful of no's worth losing your dream?

If you take the time to work through to your ultimate goal, it will be worth it!

Holly{WOULD}
Keep asking.

A messy strategy

Knowing that people were coming over for a tasting party, I messed up my house before they arrived.

When they stepped inside, I wanted them to see homework on the table and dishes in the sink. I hoped they would think, Oh, my house looks even better than hers and she's a Presidential—let's get this done!

When I noticed the looks of relief and determination on their faces, I inwardly grinned. I thought, All right! Mission accomplished!

An hour or so later, I sat down at the kitchen table with three new enrollees.

"Okay, get out your calendars and let's set some times for me to come speak at your tasting parties."

One said, "Oh, I can't yet! My house isn't ready. I have to paint my dining room!"

The second said, "I need a new coffee table. Mine is stained beyond repair!"

The third one said, "First, I need new throw pillows for my couch!"

Looking up from my calendar, I said, "Your friends saw your houses yesterday without the new paint, coffee table, and throw pillows, so ask them over and tell them to bring their friends."

They all pulled out their calendars and we set some party dates!

Then I advised, "Don't clean your houses until they're perfect. As a matter of fact, mess them up. After you've greeted your guests and poured the juice, then just start flipping the chart. You don't have to be perfect."

Holly {WOULD}
Mess it up!

In a people business, perfection is not duplicable, but mistakes and messes are. Duplicating yourself grows your business.

If you'll stand up there and mess it up, the person sitting there who is scared to death will have more confidence to get up there and talk. That person will think, "Okay, she messed up and people still got in. I can surely do it."

Confidence accepts imperfection.

The fruit doesn't fall far from the tree

Although my dad had confidence in himself, he didn't directly inspire it in me. He expected me to be perfect in every task I performed, whether in chores or in sports, so I was always trying to please him. In gymnastics from ages six through eight, I remember executing round-off back handsprings in the living room. When he walked in from work, my mom would say, "Show your dad, Holly." Afraid of failing him, I would fall on my head. I never fell on my head except when he was watching.

However, I gleaned confidence from him by watching him from a distance. I saw how people wanted to be around him because he was very positive and happy all the time. To every person around him he asked, "Hi, how are you today?" To this day, he's the kind of person who makes you feel like you're the only person in the room. I love that trait because it draws a person in and makes them feel good. I know my positive side came from watching my dad interact with people.

A confident person is a positive person.

My dad and I, December 2010. He visits us every Christmas.

Road trip! as told by Maranda

Corbin and Holly were getting ready to do a Texas business road tour—Dallas, Austin, San Antonio, Houston, and then back to Dallas.

They had just bought a motor home from Charlie Kalb, who had spent a lot of money tuning it up and making sure there wouldn't be any glitches. Both of our families decided to hit the road together, bringing our five boys on an exciting summer road trip.

The night before, Dan and I had a big group of people over to our house. We ate hamburgers and popped popcorn while we watched the movie *RV* outside. Our exotic deer came up close and watched it with us. When a deer got hit on the screen, one of our deer jumped!

Before we hit the road, we rushed to the grocery store to get a lot of food for our five boys who were always hungry.

We set out on the road, but hadn't even made it to the highway when the motor home overheated and the dash lights started flashing! We pulled over and Corbin was frustrated. The whole time, Holly was in the back making sandwiches, all positive and saying, "It'll be all right."

I was thinking, How are we going to make it to Austin for our meeting tonight? It was four to five hours down the road.

It was 105 degrees outside, and the motor home was getting hot. Corbin was able to get ahold of a motor home repair place that was only ten miles down the road, so we got back on the road. When we got there, they told us, "This is not a quick fix. We will have to pull this out, and pull that out."

Everyone but Holly started freaking out. She said, "It's all right," and started asking the mechanic, "Are you sure you don't have the part?"

A neighbor came and picked us up. We drove back to the repair shop in a Suburban pulling a sixteen-foot trailer and an Escalade. Then we had to figure out how we were going to fit the contents of a forty-five-foot motor home into two cars and a trailer. We had audiovisual equipment, all of our business tools, and ten people with luggage packed for a seven-day trip.

The kids were going nuts, running all around. Holly was calmly pulling things out of the motor home and putting them into the two cars and trailer. When we took off again, we were packed in like sardines. Holly was just laughing about it the whole time and telling us, "It's all good. They will have the motor home fixed by the time we get back. When things go haywire, a great story always comes out of it!"

We felt like the Griswold family on their cross-country road trip to Walley World theme park in the movie *Vacation*. At one point, we even pulled into the world's largest water park called Schlitterbahn in New Braunfels, Texas.

At Schlitterbahn with Dan and Maranda's family, our family, and our sitter, Emily.

When we returned to the repair shop, the motor home was not fixed. The mechanic said, "It will take three months." That was the whole summer!

Corbin and Holly rented a U-Haul truck and drove home to Tulsa. When they told Charlie about the motor home, he said, "Bring it back," and he refunded their money.

Holly can take any situation and spin it into a positive. Even though you know a situation is negative, you're okay with it because Holly is positive about it.

Look What We Get to Do!

{ C H A P T E R   1 3 }

When the football scoreboard broke down at our sons' school of a thousand students, over fifty families there had already joined the business and achieved Gold level or above. Their success changed the landscape of our private school, literally.

I met with them, and said, "Let's pitch in together and buy a big, new scoreboard for the football team!"

"Great!" they said, and everyone contributed whatever amount they chose.

I told the school, "If I'm going to do this, I'm going to advertise, of course."

Now our football field boasts a huge scoreboard with our company name and one of our favorite company mottos. Sitting at the first football game after it was unveiled, I overheard some parents who didn't know me, saying, "Can you believe that juice-business scoreboard?"

I turned around and said, "I can. You should have done it with us."

I have so much fun in this business! Jobs aren't always fun, but this is not a job. This business is about helping others, and that is what I get to do.

Spreading the opportunity

One day as we shopped in Bobbi Brown cosmetics, Emily said, "Guess what? I lost five pounds on our company's weight-loss product!"

Overhearing me, someone stopped, pivoted, and walked back to us to ask what product we were talking about!

In another store, we started talking about where we were going and what we were doing. "We'll be in Vegas soon."

The clerk waiting on us said, "What do you do?"

"We have a juice business. You need to do it with us so we can hang out!"

We told her about our upcoming company trip. "Oh, and we're going to have so much fun in Hawaii! You should do this with us."

"Oh, that sounds like so much fun!"

When we travel to Las Vegas, a group of us will get our makeup done together. It always seems bigger and better when someone else applies it.

"Are all of you out here on business or pleasure?" the makeup artists always ask.

"Yes," we always look at each other and say. Everything we do in business is fun for us.

They ask, "Well, what do you do that's fun?"

"Have you ever heard of the juice business? We're looking for people who want to build this market out here in Las Vegas. What a fun place! We come back all the time. This is a business you can do yourself as an independent distributor of a health product that's fantastic. Everyone needs it and people are making a lot of money. We have our friends with us, and one of them has a birthday today, so we have a big night out. Where's a good place to go for a birthday dinner?"

After we chat about dinner arrangements, we add, "Oh, and we're coming back in a couple of months, so you ought to come to our tasting party! Or if you want to try the product, let me have your card, and I'll send you the product."

Most of them say yes. Not all of them jump into business with us but they all get a taste of fun! On a return trip, we pick up the conversation where we left off.

Our goal is to help as many people as we can, and we have fun doing it!

Aloha!

During our annual trip to Maui with some of our best friends, we get to turn off our cell phones and relax by the beach.

Beforehand, I tell my team, "I'll be in cabana number twelve beside the pool with the company leaders on Tuesday. Come early! Grab your towels and get a chair!"

When new Diamonds arrive, we run to the front of the hotel to take their pictures for Facebook. It doesn't matter if they're a part of our team or not; we all root for each other. Everyone smothers them with attention!

Holly{WOULD}

Energize people by bringing them together.

I've been all over the world now with some of my best friends and new friends I continue to meet. On our trips, we build great relationships and great memories. We get together and laugh.

When asked about our family's travels, our eight-year-old Ethan responded:

"Ethan, what was your favorite trip so far?"

"Bahamas!"

"Did you go swimming?"

"Yeah, and slides."

"What trip are you looking forward to next?"

"Switzerland!"

When Drake, our eleven-year-old, was asked, "What do you like about the juice business," he responded, "Going on the trips and being with my family more!"

Orange Camaro

How fun would it be to get your spouse something they'd always dreamed of? Corbin had always wanted a sports car. I'm practical, so I wouldn't let him buy one.

About a week before Christmas 2009, I decided, "You know what! I'm going to get him the latest-model Camaro."

I didn't know anything about cars, but I knew "fast and loud" were important. Corbin's brother-in-law knew the owner of a car dealership, so I called that owner and said, "I want to get my husband a Camaro. I want your fastest, loudest, best car on the lot. We're Oklahoma State Cowboy fans, so I'm thinking orange and black are the perfect colors."

He said, "You know what! I bought my wife one, but she doesn't like it because it's too fast. My son super-souped it up."

I met him down at the dealership, where he said, "I think I have what you need. Do you want to take it for a test drive?"

"No, I don't know how to drive a stick. You're going to have to take me for a ride."

So we got in the car and went for a ride. I said, "Is this fast? Is this loud? I mean, will a guy get excited about this car?"

"Yes! He'll love it!"

I arranged to have it delivered in the middle of the night on Christmas day so when Corbin woke up, he would see it outside in the driveway!

Before that happened, Tulsa received its first blizzard warning in history! I panicked! How would I give Corbin his car?

During the day on Christmas eve, I called the guys at the dealership. "You're going to have to deliver it now. Drive it to my mom's garage."

They did, and as predicted, an ice storm hit that night.

Christmas eve, we all started opening presents at my mom's house. My little brother, Bret, said, "Hey Corbin, can you come out to the garage and help me bring some presents in?"

All of us followed them out there. There it was—a beautiful car with the number nineteen on it! Corbin saw it, wheeled around, and walked out of the garage, mad!

Standing next to Bo, I said, "I don't think he likes it! Now what am I going to do?"

Bo turned and said, "Hey, Corbin, what do you think of the car?"

Corbin thought Bo said, "What do you think of *my* car?" He couldn't believe Bo had bought the car he wanted.

Dakota started screaming, "Dad! Dad! It's *your* car!"

In disbelief, Corbin said, "I love it!"

Van Pelt kids and my kids beside Corbin's new orange Camaro. "Surprise!"

We couldn't distract him from it the rest of the day! While the kids kept opening presents, Corbin kept starting his, out in the garage.

During the many days it took the ice to melt off the roads, he probably burned two tanks of gas in the garage, just from starting that thing. When I wondered where Corbin was, he was always at my mom's house, in the garage, starting the car! Every day, he checked the weather to see if he could drive the car home.

I'm telling you, not only was it fun for him, but for our three little boys, who were fired up about riding in it to and from school.

Before the business, I never fulfilled a big dream for my husband. I never dreamed of giving our school a scoreboard, and I never reserved cabanas in Maui for friends.

I believe you can do this, too!

What Would Holly Do?

{ C H A P T E R   1 4 }

My good friend, Heidi, has watched me juggle family and business for years and likes to tell people that my positive attitude makes it look easy.

Holly, through Heidi's eyes

When I'm in a situation and I don't know exactly what to do, I often ask myself, "What would Holly do?"

When I'm helping someone with a problem or challenge, I ask myself, "What would Holly say?"

No matter the bumps that hit her schedule, you'll hear her say, "*Per*-fect!"

Babysitter cancels: Holly says, "Actually that's *per*-fect because the boys want to spend time with us anyway, so we'll just take them and get ice cream afterwards!"

Discovers she has to drive six hours to Des Moines: "Actually that's *per*-fect because we can get all our calls made on the road, and we can stop halfway in Kansas City and eat Minsky's pizza— Corbin has been craving it anyway! And I'll return that purchase to Anthropologie while I'm at it!"

Major event falls on Ethan's birthday: "It actually works out *per*-fect because now he gets to celebrate it twice—once with my mom and his cousins and again with us after we get back!"

Flight gets canceled and she can't make it to the big meeting where she's speaking: "It's *per*-fect because it will give our friend a chance to do her first big meeting and prove to herself that she can do it. She'll get to be seen as the leader! *Per*-fect!"

I find myself saying *per*-fect all the time! It makes life easier and it's the quickest way to a solution!

Looking out for you

Heidi continues:

Holly is a careful observer. I have seen her notice when a person is struggling or down and be the first to step in. When she sees someone isolating themselves, she is quick to pull them into the shelter of the group. She plans social activities, get-togethers and team meetings.

I copy her by regularly getting people on my team together to build relationships that hopefully will sustain them through the ebb and flow of business.

Holly is quick to give recognition for accomplishments. She gives others credit for their great ideas.

She never speaks poorly of others or gossips. If she has to relay something factual that reflects poorly on people, she always follows it with something positive:

"...but they have had a lot going on in their lives."

"...they are great people who just got off track a little."

"...they've learned a ton by making that mistake."

"...they are sharp and won't let this get them down."

I wasn't much of a gossiper before, but I have taken this to heart and now *refuse* to gossip in business or in my personal life. Holly set the example for me in this area.

When Steve and I moved to Kansas City to be closer to our family, Holly said to me over and over, "*Be bold!* Be confident in your company and proud of what you've built!"

She also said, "*You* are the leaders," which helped us see ourselves in a new light and enabled us to step up to the plate in our city. She guided us where we needed it and continued to encourage us as we improved.

Holly {WOULD}
Encourage.

Holly digs positives out of the most negative situations. Shortly after we settled into our home in Kansas City, my dad had to have a kidney removed and open heart surgery. They lived in a tiny town almost two hours from the best hospital in KC. Because we now lived in KC, Mom and Dad were able to stay with us while he recovered and be near doctors and the hospital. While there was nothing fun about that time, Holly was the first to point out how amazing God was for getting us to KC just in time to help my parents and make that time easier for them. I was able to be with them instead of driving back and forth from Tulsa to help.

I now copy that brand of thinking when I am talking with my friends. I try to point out how God is working in their tough situations. This is powerful thinking that helps us feel thankful during tough times.

Holly {WOULD}
Thank God.

In Holly's eyes, people are potential. She is great at helping people imagine *big* things:

"Your team will have the most people at the event."

"Your team can take over that ship on the free trip."

"I've never seen so much fire in your team!"

She helps us picture what we want to happen so we can make it happen.

Holly makes things happen! She doesn't wait around for someone to decide to do things—she boldly asks for what she wants. When we are planning a big meeting, she has taught us to call the company and ask for free product or giveaways, or for a lower ticket price, or for a Black Diamond to come speak in our area. It never hurts to ask, even if they say no.

She convinced the company to hold the Black Diamond trip at a hotel in Cabo San Lucas where she has always wanted to visit; to use her favorite color—orange—for their new weight-loss product line; and to hold their next major event in the location of her choice.

Connie, Holly's mother says: "Holly isn't afraid to ask. I don't know where she gets it from because I would totally be the opposite. Most people wouldn't do that, but it doesn't bother her. I think she thinks of it as doing them a favor; it's an honor for them to get to do this."

Holly {WOULD}

Ask because she's doing *you* a favor!

Intimidated? Not me!

When Bo was a rookie on the PGA tour, Carrie and Corbin and I went to one of his tournaments in Milwaukee. Afterward, we went to Chicago together.

Sitting in our hotel lobby, we noticed that a new ESPN Zone across the street was getting ready to throw a grand-opening VIP party. Only personally invited professional athletes and movie stars could attend. We could see employees rolling out the red carpet, so I eagerly anticipated a celebrity sighting. I said, "Bo, you're a professional athlete. You should get to go."

Bo said, "Holly, nobody even knows me. I'm the rookie on tour. I'm not going to get into that party."

That didn't stop me. When I saw one of the Zone's security guards walking through our lobby, I approached him. Pointing to our small group, I said, "We want to go to the party. My brother-in-law sitting over there is on the PGA tour. His name is Bo Van Pelt."

The guard said, "Who?"

I said, "When you go back, tell the ESPN Zone that Bo Van Pelt is here and would like to attend your party."

He took Bo's cell phone number and said, "We're going to check it out and then we'll call you."

Sure enough, he called and said, "We checked it out. You're welcome to attend."

We walked the red carpet into the party! Free food and drinks were everywhere, as well as rigged games to enjoy. As movie stars entered, announcers proclaimed them by name as "in the house!" We saw the Chicago Bears team who had won the Super Bowl and met an NFL quarterback.

Then, we found out there was a VIP party within that VIP party, so I told Bo, "Show them your PGA Tour card. The worst they can say is no." And that's how we got into that party!

Years ago, I got into Fashion Week in New York City by acting confident in line. I had always wanted to attend a fashion show, and Corbin and I were in Times Square where it was being held near Valentine's Day. I told Corbin, "Act like you know what you are doing. You are supposed to be here!" We just walked right into the famous show.

Passionate confidence gets you places!

Holly, through Jill's eyes

I've known Holly for twelve years, since our oldest boys were two, before the juice company existed. We lived in the same neighborhood for a while, and she was always prepared, always up, always ready for the next thing.

One day she pulled into the cul-de-sac with the boys in the little red Radio Flyer wagon. I said, "Are you excited for your trip to Aruba?"

"Yes, it's next week. I'm already packed!"

Who packs a week before a trip? I said, "Oh that's great. I'm leaving on a trip tomorrow and I haven't even thought about what I'm wearing."

She is great about thinking forward to the next month, and even out to the next two holidays. She plans way out on her calendar, which is probably partly why she is confident. She knows where she is and where she is going.

Holly {WOULD}
Think ahead.

When she says she's going to do something, she does it. Way back, Holly decided to diet and she stuck to it. She looked great! The diet included an exercise plan with a twenty-minute run. She followed it all to a tee. She disciplined herself very well to follow the whole thing.

Holly {WOULD}
Carry out a decision.

Holly makes quick decisions. I asked her interior decorator how Holly's house was decorated so quickly, and she said Holly decides quickly. She trusts her decisions.

Holly{WOULD}
Decide quickly.

She is very good about delegating. One time I heard her raspy voice on the end of the phone, saying, "Jill, you have to take this meeting for me. I can't talk."

I was very nervous, but I did it. Holly told me I could do it. "You'll do fine. Just do it, don't worry about it. Don't think too hard about it."

Holly{WOULD}
Delegate.

Holly can multitask like no one else. I've seen her talk to Dallin while pointing me toward something while walking toward someone else. She is queen of the multitaskers.

Holly{WOULD}
Multitask.

Calm during the storm

Emily, Jill, and Katie recall a time when Holly stayed calm during chaos around her:

Holly negotiated a room at a hotel for her big meeting. We set up the room and then went to dinner. When we returned, someone had stolen all the audio-visual equipment. Not only that, but more than double the people we expected started pouring into the room.

We had to completely scramble to set up more chairs! Before dinner, we had centered the chairs facing the stage. But now, we had to add more chairs, then more, then more and more. We rushed to move this, move that, spread chairs, move everything around, and it had to happen like *that!* We were rushing so much, we sounded like we were hyperventilating!

Our own seats, which were originally in front and center, ended up down at the end of a row. We even had to open up a temporary wall to make more room. When we started the meeting, we literally found ourselves in two full rooms instead of one.

Katie: "If I were in Holly's shoes, I would have fallen apart. Because of the way we had to keep adding more chairs, it was so funny how that room kept growing: *Shift! Shift! Shift!*"

Jill: "While we were panicking, Holly kept saying, *"How great! How great! How great!"*

Holly {WOULD}
Remain calm in chaos.

Q & A with Emily, Jill, and Katie

Q: If a new contact said no to your business, what would Holly say if you called her to complain about it?

Emily: "We don't call Holly to complain. She's definitely gained that respect from us. But when others tell her about a negative experience, first, she definitely gives a sympathetic 'Aw...that's bad,' and then she changes it to a positive by saying:

Jill: 'Find somebody else.'

Katie: 'Make one more call because you may have just had a bad call. But if you make one or two more, you're probably going to find someone who's interested.'

Emily: 'In this business, all we need to do is keep putting new people in. New people are the fire of the business.'"

Q: What more can you add about the way Holly thinks?

Katie: "Holly does not listen to negativity. Holly conditions people to think positively. We have learned to think the way Holly thinks, and the way she thinks has made her successful. We have learned what she would say to people."

Emily: "When you've been around Holly enough, you don't have to call her as much for advice. When I'm dealing with something, I just think, 'What would Holly say?' And I find my answer very fast."

Q: What would Holly say, for example?

Katie: "I had a young lady call me who had a problem with someone in her business. She wanted to call the person and give her a piece of her mind.

"I said, 'You know, I don't think that's going to do what you think it's going to do. I don't think you're going to have a good outcome.'

"She said, "Well, this is what I think I'm going to do.

"I said, 'This is not what Holly Roush would do. Maybe you don't respect me, but I know you respect Holly.'"

"Holly would have told her, 'Focus on the positive areas of your business. Don't focus on the negative and bring everybody down.'"

Jill: "She doesn't hold a grudge with her family or friends. She just moves forward."

Emily: "She chooses to think about the positive. It's a lot about choices for her."

Jill: "I learned from her to just try to find the positive in the negative. When she knows a negative situation is not within her forte, she is good at pointing people to different resources."

Katie: "She keeps her eyes on priorities."

Q: What more can you tell me about Holly's confident traits?

Emily: "She sees things coming. She knows that things will cough up, so if she has a minute now to do something that she knows about, then when something pops up, she'll be prepared and it won't stress her out."

Katie: "She used to call me and ask me if I would do things like call a restaurant to see if they had a private room. By the time I would get to it, she would already have done it herself."

Jill: "She attacks things."

Holly{WOULD}

Get it done.

Emily: "She's definitely smart and tactical. Everyone has excuses about why they can't. With boxes everywhere the day before they moved, she threw a tasting party."

Katie: "She had another tasting party the night before she left for Europe."

Holly{WOULD}
Make a way.

Emily: "She can read a room like you would not believe."

Katie: "She is incredibly into them. She reads body language and expressions."

Emily: "At a meeting, she'll say, 'Emily, come up and talk about the product.' And as you're talking, you can see her beside you scanning the crowd, judging how in tune they are. If they start glazing over, she wraps it up by saying, 'Okay, good. All right, thanks.'"

Holly{WOULD}
Keep everyone's attention.

Katie: "Every phone call from Holly is an accountability meeting. When I first got started, because she personally enrolled me, she would call me every couple of days and check on me: 'Do you have your list? Have you talked to people?' I realized she was going to keep calling, so I thought, I have to start calling people!

"She keeps you on top of things. We have a general calendar we all go to on Holly and Corbin's Web site and her mother, Connie, posts all of our meetings there. It really all comes down to principles of success, such as consistency, persistence, and doing something every day. If you're not following those principles, then you're not going to build your business and you're not going to be confident in your ability to succeed. So Holly's accountability is to make sure we're following the principles."

Holly {WOULD}
Keep people accountable.

Jill: "Initially, Holly could have told me, 'This is how much money you can make, and this product is the best thing in the world,' and still, I would have just said, 'Okay great, that's awesome,' and then I would have left it if it wasn't for her. Holly engaged us. She was excited about the juice.

"She's an organizer and extremely sociable. In the neighborhood, Holly and Corbin would always throw cool parties. When I would drive into the cul-de-sac and see a massive amount of cars, I would think, Oh my gosh, Holly's throwing another party!"

Katie: "She doesn't want to have four people over. She wants to have twenty."

Jill: "She doesn't have to, but she always brings everyone together. Barbecue at her house, lunches together, houseboat parties, summers on the lake, Christmas parties. She loves to get us together to dance in her family room or play Guitar Hero."

My fortieth birthday party, Rock of Ages theme at Carrie and Bo Van Pelt's home, July 19, 2010.

Katie: "Probably one of the key things that has kept us going is socializing together."

Holly{WOULD}
Organize fun times for her team.

Katie: "If you look at what the Roushs have come into and what they've been able to do, and then you look at their kids, it's amazing how grounded they are. They are good boys!

"Holly and Corbin are open with them about why they do what they do, so the boys know their parents are helping other families get to the same position in life.

"They could sit back and do nothing and live very comfortably. But they know that families are out there who still need their help, and that's what keeps pushing them.

"We never think that they are selfishly going after things. Yes, we all want to make more money, and yes, that's important, but Holly and Corbin want to do the right things with their money—they tithe, they save, and they give."

$\mathcal{Holly}${WOULD}
Keep going for the good of others.

Emily: "Every day, she's on the phone with someone new in the business and giving them advice on how to get their business started. When we travel by plane, every time I walk into an airport, she's already on her phone, saying, 'Okay, the first thing you want to do is put one person on your left and one person on your right. Then teach them to do the same.'"

Katie: "When we traveled, I always said, 'Okay, I need to hear you talking to people. I need to hear how you handle things.' She would take a call, turn to me, and say, 'Did that help?'

"One day, we made a three-way call. After the person we called hung up, she said, 'Okay, do you think you can do it that way?'

"That time, I said, 'Yes,' but I was thinking, It's actually the way I already do it, but she can do it better."

Q: *What makes her better?*

Jill: "She knows without a shadow of a doubt that this is *the* opportunity for people. And when she presents it, you know she knows."

Katie: "She's just so confident and passionate about it! She was that way even when she didn't know anything about it. I call her a freak of nature."

Holly, through Katie's eyes

What I learned from Holly is that negativity pulls people down. I learned to get over complaining about other people or situations and I learned to put on big-girl panties if I wanted to grow my business and hang with the people who were making it happen.

The most important lesson I learned was that people who speak badly about others often have a bigger problem within themselves, and instead of being concerned with what other people are doing or saying, they need to look in the mirror and work on what's inside of them before greatness can happen. That's not an easy lesson.

In this business, what goes around comes around. So whatever struggle you are having now, someone in your business will have the same struggles down the road and you will be faced with managing issues that perhaps in the past you might have caused. Having the tide turned on you takes personal growth to a new level!

In tough situations I began to ask, "What would Holly do?" It changed my whole outlook and I became a happier person.

Thank you!

No one succeeds without the help of others. Something I love about this community commerce business is the opportunity to help each other succeed.

Time for a New You!

Starting out in any industry, people usually have a lot of questions about whether or not they're going to be able to succeed. That's called counting the cost and considering the opportunity.

Who would want to open a business on a whim, saying, "Hey, I think I'll open up a coffee shop tomorrow"? We're confident when we research the details.

People frequently ask, "If I decide to get started in business, will the time commitment hurt my family?"

I respond, "That's where priorities and personal development intertwine."

All yours

Guard specific times when you will be available to your spouse and children. That may mean turning off your phone. It took me a long time to do that because I thought I had to be all things to all people. I thought, What if someone really needs me? What if someone has a pressing question?

I learned that people are fine an hour later when I call them back. I learned to relax in the thought, Right now, this is my family time.

More than tons of time, our kids and spouses need quality time. Prioritized time is quality time because it is undistracted time. I try to arrange my day by what can help my family the most. Prioritizing this way prevents little things from stealing my whole day.

To prioritize your day, ask yourself, What can benefit my family? What can help move us toward our goals?

Be sensible, only saying yes to things that will benefit your family the most. You might have to learn to say no to some things. Make some short-term decisions for your long-term future.

Prior to a new day, I organize my thoughts. I feel much better the next morning when I have listed my priorities the night before. That way, I don't go to bed with confusing thoughts that wake me up at night. When the alarm goes off, I'm ready to go!

Focusing on your priorities will build your confidence!

I could share my product and build my team 24/7, but Corbin watches me and pulls me into balance by saying, "Remember, this is the kids' time." I would probably be a workaholic, but he brings me back to family.

Ten-minute meals

Mothers know how important it is to feed our families healthful meals. Even so, the National Prevention Council's June 2011 report states that "fewer than 15 percent of adults and 10 percent of adolescents eat recommended amounts of fruit and vegetables each day."[1]

Always on the go with our sons' sports, Corbin and I would throw fast-food to them in the backseat of our car, and say, "Hurry!

Eat it, eat it!" Their daily portion of fruit came from the filling in pop tarts—"Today you get strawberry, tomorrow blueberry..."

Feeling guilty, every Sunday I thought, Today is the day—I'm going to the grocery store and buying a variety of fruits and vegetables and we're going to start eating right!

In spite of my best intentions, we never did, which was one reason I was so excited about the juice that fulfills our daily fruit requirements in only four ounces a day!

If your family keeps a fast pace, but you enjoy cooking, find recipes that are simple and convenient. It's comforting to stop and realize that children don't even notice how much time you put into preparation of a meal, so why should you invest a lot of time or ingredients?

I don't love to cook, but I know my family has to be fed and I'm going to serve what they like so that they'll eat it. I try to do it in a healthful way, but if I have to serve takeout, I have to serve takeout. We don't eat perfectly, but we never go without a meal.

Continuing education

Do you think you aren't smart enough to step into business because you struggled to get A's and didn't earn a college degree?

I wasn't book smart. I had to work hard for every grade. My high-school sophomore math teacher told my mom that I would never make it through college because I was way too sociable. I did like to talk in class!

My Spanish One teacher told me, "Please don't come see me for Spanish Two." Since I'm a visual learner, I had a hard time hearing the language. I just couldn't process it.

Good grades don't necessarily bring the most success in life. I think what college provides is a network of people and proves that you're tenacious enough to be on your own and still make your grades for four years, but I don't know how much it helps you down the road to success in *every* industry. In my industry, many of the successful businesspeople do not have a college degree and some who have one tend to overthink unnecessary details.

I loved college, and I'll highly recommend it to my kids. Since people have all of their lives to work, I think they should enjoy college, network, and make friends! I definitely learned more social and organizational skills because I was off on my own and had to study on my own. Something I definitely learned from college was time management. My sorority taught me that.

When a teacher called me about one of my sons being too sociable, I wasn't very worried about it. I thought, I'm okay with sociable as long as he isn't disrupting the class—which he wasn't.

When asked to picture a time when they faced a hard test at school and to recall the advice I gave them, Dakota said, "Try your hardest"; Drake said, "Put in your 110 percent"; and Ethan said, "Try your hardest every time!"

It's the same in business, too. Pick yourself up and try.

So many people are afraid of failure. To me, you aren't failing if you're trying. Failure is not making an effort. If you're making an effort to fulfill your dreams, and along the way you experience setbacks, those setbacks are learning experiences, not failures. Every setback I've ever had has turned into a way for me to understand and help others, and your setbacks will turn into the exact experiences that will help people you know in business.

In my industry, some of our biggest leaders are ones who have been in business for four years. Not three months, four years.

They've stuck to it, they know business growth involves a learning process, and they know they're growing personally.

I'm confident when I believe in something very strongly; strongly enough to dive into it and learn more about it. It's worth getting a little more in depth and even worth failing a little bit as I learn.

Confidence is when you believe in something so strongly that you don't need to know every detail in advance, knowing it will come over time.

Beauty is as beauty does

My industry, as most industries, does not discriminate according to looks. Inherited physical traits mean nothing; confidence means everything. It doesn't matter what you look like; it matters how you feel about yourself. Some of the most beautiful people are insecure.

Confidence is all about how you carry yourself.

If you carry yourself like you're unhappy with the way you look, then that unhappiness is what people will see when they look at you. If you carry yourself in a way that says, I'm feeling good, I'm looking good, and I love what I do, people will be excited to see you.

On the chunky side growing up, I was teased for my weight. My maternal grandmother would say, "Oh, Holly, you look healthy! You're just big boned." Kids would comment about my size, too, and I remember dieting in elementary school.

Knowing that none of us were built exactly the same, I think God gave us the attributes we have and we need to bring out the

best in them. We all have something great to offer, and we all motivate people in a different way through our uniqueness.

Holly{WOULD}
Feel good about her imperfect self.

I tell people dress for success. In college, when I woke up in the morning facing a final exam, I learned not to just roll out of bed and show up to take it. I learned to apply some makeup, style my hair, and put on an outfit I felt cute in because then I felt confident walking in to take the test. I felt good about myself when I took the time to take care of myself.

What makes you feel confident?

One of my favorite things to do is work out because it makes me feel good and I'm doing something for myself. It boosts my confidence in talking to people.

We need to give our spouses time for themselves, too. Doing something special for them is important, like the time I scheduled a massage for Corbin with a lady who comes to her customer's houses. I told him, "Don't schedule anything from 1:00 p.m. to 2:00 p.m." He deserved it.

When someone was nervous about appearing in the company's magazine and video, I said, "You know what, go treat yourself. Buy nice shirts that both you and your spouse feel good in. Doing that will build your confidence and it will show! Rather than going into your closet and looking for a staple that you don't feel fun in, do what makes you feel confident and excited."

Remember this: It's how you carry yourself that matters.

Opening up

If you feel that personal shyness is a deterrent to starting or developing your business, first of all, don't feel badly about yourself. So many of us now tend to hide behind our computers rather than come out and face the big world.

If you realize you don't have friends, that's okay, because now you recognize a personal weakness and you know what to work on to build your business. Since businesses serve people, you have to know people to be in business and to grow one.

Part of having friends is being confident enough to be friendly, to reach out and touch people. Dive into some social circles. If you like to exercise, join a workout class. If you like to study the Bible, join a Bible study. If you're a mom, find a Mother's Day Out group where you can get to know other moms and your children can play together.

Are you thinking, I don't have the money to join these kinds of groups?

Well, go for a walk outside and start talking to your neighbors. Churches are free, and many even offer free coffee where people can talk and get to know one another.

Maybe you need to read the famous book, *How to Win Friends & Influence People* by Dale Carnegie. Feed yourself in the area of your biggest weakness, and go make some friends.

Holly{WOULD}

Feed herself in the areas
where she is weak.

Start somewhere.

I know a lot of shy people who had never invited people to join them in anything before starting their business. Through passion for their product, they have pushed past that obstacle to build their business. And good news—many of them have found talkative friends who do most of the talking for them!

The right approach

No matter what industry you go into, don't be afraid to approach people who are successful in it and ask them questions.

My whole life, I've been a sponge! I look for people who have characteristics I like and I place myself around them to listen to their advice. When I go to any kind of business event or on trips the company provides, I stay around the highest leaders in the business and I listen to them as they interact with people. I listen to their advice.

Be a big listener!

I believe, you don't know unless you ask. Always ask and then listen. If I'm unsure about something, I have no problem asking. It's important to go straight to the source, to the person who can give the information you need.

To develop confidence and retain it, you have to be willing to hear about your imperfections and how you can improve, and then develop those skills you lack, whether by reading a book or going to a seminar or getting around somebody who is better in those areas.

Personal growth is one of the great benefits of being in business.

When it comes to your product, who knows the moment when someone will need it? Don't be afraid to approach people about the benefits of your business.

As my business grew, I learned not to let the six inches between my ears keep me from excluding anyone. I didn't prejudge them according to whether I thought they made too much money, they had small children, they were too busy, they had a job, or they didn't have enough money. I wrote down everyone I could think of.

What if Bo's friend hadn't told him about the juice? If Butter had skipped him because he thought, Oh, Bo would never be interested because he's a PGA golfer on the road all the time, then Corbin and I wouldn't be in this business. My sister, Carrie, and her husband, Bo, are Black Diamonds now and are the reason a lot of people are in this juice business today. We are grateful to them for introducing us to the opportunity.

My sister, Carrie, and her husband, Bo, at their lake house on Grand Lake in Oklahoma, Thanksgiving weekend 2009.

Never prejudge. Tell people and let them decide for themselves.

Confident people don't prejudge who needs what they have.

Who is a confident person? A confident person:

- has a dream
- works to fulfill that dream
- is willing to fight for that dream
- accepts constructive criticism
- works to improve weaknesses
- turns negatives into positives

1. (http://www.healthcare.gov/center/councils/nphpphc/strategy/report.pdf).

You Can Do It!

{ C H A P T E R   1 6 }

The first time I spoke onstage at a business meeting, Brig gave me about twenty minutes. As I walked out to face the crowd, suddenly I experienced a serious case of cottonmouth. My lips were stuck to my teeth!

If that has ever happened to you, you know I was dying!

Desperately, I looked for help. I knew my team was watching me on the giant screen and I was thinking, Surely they notice me trying to open my mouth. Why isn't anyone helping me?

My only alternative was to talk as well as I could without completely opening my mouth, and I probably cut my allotted time by five minutes. I had to get off that stage! Amazingly, people said to me, "Man, I never knew you could speak that well."

From that experience, I learned to drink a lot of water beforehand and to bring some water with me. But if I had never gotten up there, I never would have known. Now what's interesting is at every event, I always make sure the speaker has water! I want to make sure they have a great experience.

I get nervous every time I speak, but not because I fear cottonmouth any longer. I get nervous because I hope to say something that touches somebody out there. If I can just affect one person, I've done my job.

Speaking to over eight thousand onstage at National Convention in Salt Lake City, Utah, June 2011.

Becoming confident in a new business is like learning to ride a bike. Be kind to yourself; set realistic expectations at each stage in your business. At first, expect less than later on. Don't discourage yourself like the kindergartner who stares upward at the high school senior and thinks, I'll never get there!

No one jumps from kindergarten to twelfth grade!

To succeed in anything—as a husband, wife, parent, or businessperson—takes confidence. Confidence means believing in yourself. If you don't believe you can succeed, how are you ever going to make it? How will you encourage others? Who's going to believe in you and your product if you don't believe?

When it comes to building confidence, people die slow deaths within when they stop diving into confidence-building activities. Here's how to get started in building your confidence, as it parallels building a business:

(1) **Invest in yourself.**

To identify where you typically gain confidence, ask yourself some questions: *Where have I felt very good about myself and about what I'm doing?* Find that place, the place that builds you up instead of brings you down and go to it over and over again. *What people were with me at that time?* Surround yourself with those people. *What was I doing when I felt encouraged?* If you were reading a book, what about it motivated you?

(2) **Keep investing in yourself until doing so becomes automatic.**

Making an initial investment in yourself and your business isn't enough. Investing in yourself is something you need to do month after month, not only once and you're done. If last month a self-improvement book helped you gain confidence personally and professionally, go get another one this month. Keep building your confidence until it becomes a habit.

(3) **Stretch yourself a little—connect with people personally and professionally.**

Putting yourself around positive, excited people and listening to their stories will uplift you and build your confidence. It's so much better than sitting in a house listening to your own uncertain or self-condemning thoughts. I love what Brig says because it's true— reading, listening, and participating help people a great deal.

Set yourself into a confidence-building routine. I promise, if you do what's important to you and what makes you feel good, the rest of your day will fall into place. You'll probably feel more energy, more motivation, better about yourself, and a little kick in your step.

And all of a sudden that business phone call isn't quite so hard to make, and talking to someone in person isn't hard at all.

Blown out of proportion

I used to stress-out in my meetings about little things, like sign-in sheets that didn't look professional.

A week before Brig and Dallin came to Tulsa for my first big meeting, a friend of mine heard them speak in Dallas. There she saw them drinking juice straight out of the bottles. She was horrified, and so was I when she told me!

I called Tim, the man I contacted about attending my first meeting in Dallas where I met Brig. "Tim, you have to call Brig. You have to tell him and Dallin they cannot drink out of the bottle when they come to my meeting in Tulsa. And another thing. Brig cannot show his wallet. That big stack of money is really turning people off! Oh, and one more thing—take off all that jewelry. That won't work in the Midwest."

Before they arrived in Tulsa, Dallin heard I was worried about the two of them drinking out of the bottles. I'll never forget what he did.

As he started walking onstage, he grabbed a bottle and started acting like he was going to drink out of it. He said, "I heard Holly doesn't like us drinking out of the bottles, so here's for you, Holly!"

Thinking he was serious, I started running up the middle aisle to the front, saying, "Look, here are some cups!"

There I was, new to this business, but thinking I had all the answers!

Dallin and Brig didn't correct me that day. I'm sure they shared a good chuckle about it, and that's fine because I'm still standing!

Being in this business for a while has helped me realize that the things I tended to become overanxious about were things that didn't really matter. It has taught me to focus on individuals instead: Is that person smiling? Am I making that one feel good? Is that person excited when she leaves here?

Like Rick Warren says in his book, *Purpose Driven Life,* if you leave people feeling good about themselves, they will be drawn to you again. When someone has spent time with you, either they'll walk away and never want to come back or they'll want to be around you again.

Don't sweat the small stuff; focus only on what is within your control.

Holly {WOULD}
Focus on giving people a good experience.

Coming and going

Some days, even confident people contend with self-doubt. In business, no one is exempt from disappointments. Businesses lose customers.

Corbin and I lost some people who said hurtful things on their way out: "They're all about themselves. All they care about is money." That hurt. A part of me thought, Am I really that way?

I knew their words weren't true, but they shook me for a minute. When other people on our team asked what happened, I said, "They just moved in a different direction," and then I looked for the silver lining.

If you know what you're doing is on the straight and narrow, when customers leave your business, it won't matter in the long run. Always the new kid growing up, I could have chosen to let loss bother me and never have come out to play. Instead, I decided to try to get to know the other kids, and if someone didn't warm up to me, I thought, Maybe she isn't the friend for me. Maybe I'll find another one.

Likewise, in business, keep your eye out for your next customer!

We all learn on the go through experiences—no regrets! Adversity is a stepping-stone. Life's struggles teach us what we can do and what we can handle. And now I can say to hurting people, "I've been there."

One thing I always pray for is to stay stable and grounded and true. None of us can change the past. I prefer to face forward.

Holly{WOULD}
Keep looking forward.

To stay energized in business, take yourself back to the place or person or story that launched you in business in the first place. It will remind you of what drives you and you will feel re-energized. Every day, Corbin and I get a phone call or an e-mail saying thank you. I like to recall the family who lost 420 pounds collectively, who now has confidence for a brighter future. That is a success I can't measure!

Staying grateful

What matters most is not the people who leave but the people who stay. That's true not only in business, but in life.

My fourth grade teacher took the time to inspire confidence in me. I had a hard time with reading comprehension, and still today, my mind sometimes wanders.

She would sit down with me, set goals, and reward me. "Holly, if you read this and take this test, then I'm going to give you this bookmark with a scratch-and-sniff sticker," she said.

After I read two books and took the test, she took me to McDonald's for a milkshake. I guess rewards were the positive reinforcement I needed!

And then I had Aunt Kathy, my mom's sister. She is my godmother. When I was little, she was great about listening and responding to me openly and honestly. She went Diamond in our business.

She tells people, "I remember when Holly's father and mother assigned me as her godmother. I worried about how I could afford to raise her along with my own kids if something happened to them. But who would have thought that now Holly is taking care of me?"

Because of our business, my aunt and uncle paid off their house and paid off their car. They're making more than they ever dreamed!

My Aunt Kathy and Uncle Scott from Bismarck, North Dakota, on a dream vacation for free with our company leaders and new Diamonds in Maui, August 2011.

Look what confidence does!

Corbin used to be so worried when I first started in the business. I remember him saying to me, "Man! All our friends are gonna run from us!"

Guess what? They run to us! When we walk in our school, they come to us and say, "Sit down with us. We want what you have. We want to work out together as a couple. We want to take our kids to school together. We want to go on their field trips." Or we hear, "I want to coach my child's soccer team, but you know what? My job ties me down, so I can't."

Once you decide to commit to a business, dive in! Don't over-think it. That's what I did, and I am so glad I did!

Over the years, people have asked me, "How do you and Corbin go out and do this every day?"

I immediately think, What? This is the best thing we've ever done! How can we not?

Our ride has been amazing, and we're just getting started. We're just now opening in a lot of countries. Our business has expanded so much that we get to stay home or drive or board a plane to hang out with our friends, some of whom we haven't seen in years.

We get to make new friends. We get to walk into rooms of excited, happy people and see their smiling faces. If we sat at home every night of the week, we would feel like the most selfish people on the planet.

We haven't neglected each other or our children—our sons are engaged in the business with us and we get to spend an ample amount of quality time together. We keep reaching goals together and we keep enjoying company-paid vacation destinations as a family. On some vacations, the company even gives each couple twelve hundred dollars to spend!

Corbin and I have had the privilege of helping twelve people become millionaires just in our team alone. We've helped seven of our friends walk away from their jobs and go into business full time with their spouses.

In the beginning all I wanted was a hundred dollars a week for manicures and pedicures and now my nails sometimes look terrible. Of course when they do, I just choose not to look at them and laugh about it!

You know what my "why" is now? I want all my friends' husbands who want to retire to be able to do so. I'm tired of seeing men and women who want to be home with their children working sixty and seventy hours a week so one day when they hit retirement age they can be home. Sadly, that will be when they won't have much time left to enjoy it.

This business has given me a new perspective on life. Corbin and I don't have to go out every night of the week, but we want to in order to see:

- dads working fewer hours away from their families

- dads who get laid off from their jobs finding comfort in knowing they have a backup plan

- families sitting together around their dinner tables

- children becoming more positive in school

I've seen so many husbands and wives grow apart because they're running in a hundred different directions. Let's get back to the family. Let's spend time together, building relationships with our children and making God and family a priority! Let's break the cycle of separation and find a common interest that brings and keeps families together!

Confidence grows through unselfish effort and a strong why. In your business, stay passionate, stay committed, and your business will grow roots. Are you passionate? Do you know you have a great thing? That's confidence!

Confidence is when you're willing to give something you believe in a try, even if it isn't widely accepted by people you care about. Confidence is a bold, strong, focused desire to do your best. Confidence is using the gifts and abilities God gave you, finding your passion, and excelling at it. Even if you fall down along the way, *a confident you* will keep getting back up!

Confidence brings wealth. Confidence brings power. Confidence brings beneficial relationships.

I want you to see your dreams come true, and I really believe with all my heart that you can make that happen. As you do, believe in yourself and help others along the way. Helping others is the most rewarding accomplishment of all!

Remember, it is better to give than to receive. If you give and inspire passionately, you will be rewarded in so many amazing ways!

You can do it!

Spending the day with my family in Tulsa, Oklahoma, September 2011. Photo taken by our friend, Monica Woodham, at her family's ranch, Hall E. Wood stables.

Confident Holly Would:

Act on her personal convictions!

Think "outside the office."

Flip conventional thinking.

Learn as business grows.

Be bold.

Nudge people outside their comfort zones.

Pursue value without fear.

Love teamwork!

Keep her eyes on the bigger picture.

Listen to the top to get to the top.

Dream big!

Duplicate herself.

Focus on you, not on herself.

Keep trying through the embarrassment.

Build relationships everywhere.

Share the benefits.

Take action.

Build a group of great people.

Pursue her passion.

Expect a yes.

See her children as a reason, not as an excuse.

Include her children.

Expect her family to care about others.

Fit business into the nooks and crannies of the day.

Surround herself with positive people.

Turn a negative into a positive.

Keep running hard and having fun!

Give people a break.

Keep going despite negative words!

Never get stuck on the no's.

Keep asking.

Mess it up!

Energize people by bringing them together.

Encourage.

Thank God.

Ask because she's doing *you* a favor!

Think ahead.

Carry out a decision.

Decide quickly.

Delegate.

Multitask.

Remain calm in chaos.

Get it done.

Make a way.

Keep everyone's attention.

Keep people accountable.

Organize fun times for her team.

Keep going for the good of others.

Feel good about her imperfect self.

Feed herself in the areas where she is weak.

Focus on giving people a good experience.

Keep looking forward.

About the Author

After six years as a stay-at-home mom, Holly Roush found an amazing career! In less than two years, she built a multimillion-dollar business and became one of the most successful people in the home-based-business world.

Every year, Holly speaks in front of thousands of people around the world encouraging them to discover and pursue their strengths, gifts, and talents.

Holly believes you were born for greatness—dream big because you deserve it! Through pursuing your passion, surrounding yourself with positive people who are fulfilling their dreams, and remembering that giving is more rewarding than receiving, you can live the meaningful life of your dreams.

Holly and her husband, Corbin, are raising their three sons, Dakota, Drake, and Ethan. They currently reside in Tulsa, Oklahoma.

Author Contact Information

To purchase books, for more information,
or to schedule Holly Roush to speak,
please contact her at:

www.HollyWould.biz

info@HollyWould.biz

CPSIA information can be obtained at www.ICGtesting.com
Printed in the USA
BVOW06s2158080416

443177BV00012B/156/P